THE
LOST
CHILD

Marietta Jaeger

Pickering Paperbacks

First Published 1983
by Pickering & Inglis,
3 Beggarwood Lane,
Basingstoke, Hants RG23 7LP,
United Kingdom

Designed by Carole B. Parrish
Edited by Judith E. Markham

ISBN: 0 7208 0554 6

Printed and bound in Great Britain by
Richard Clay (The Chaucer Press) Ltd, Bungay, Suffolk

NO TRACE FOUND OF MISSING GIRL

SEARCH WIDENS FOR GIRL, 7, FEARED KIDNAPPED

RANCHERS CALLED ON TO AID IN SEARCH FOR MISSING CHILD

JAEGER FAMILY RETURNS FROM MONTANA—WITHOUT SUSIE

These are just a few of the hundreds of headlines that filled newspapers nationwide in June 1973 when Susie Jaeger, age 7, disappeared in the middle of the night, while she and her family were on a camping vacation in Montana.

THE LOST CHILD is a first-person account told by Susie's mother, Marietta Jaeger, as she re-calls the kidnapping of her youngest daughter and the ensuing sixteen months until the case was solved.

THE LOST CHILD reads like a suspense novel as it chronicles the nationwide search for the missing child and for clues to the identity of the person or persons behind her disappearance. But this is much more than a mystery story.

THE LOST CHILD is a powerful modern-day parable of faith and forgiveness as it also tells the story of Marietta Jaeger's spiritual journey through fear, terror, anger, and grief into the light of belief in a personal, loving, and merciful God.

To Susie —— safely home

Life so brief, yet filled with grace
Touching all who saw your face.
Child of God, beyond all need,
For the grieving intercede.

> *from "Child of Light"*
> *—Candace Colborn*

Contents

Acknowledgments

With deepest gratitude, I would like to acknowledge my editor, Judy Markham, for her patience and much-needed expertise; Mary Ann Feathers Lenahan, who generously volunteered to type my final manuscript; and Karen, my treasured friend, and all my sisters and brothers in the Lord who so faithfully loved, encouraged, and prayed me through the living and the writing of this story.

Introduction

As I wrote this book, I thought of it as "Susie's Story"; and yet it is really my story. It is the story of my spiritual journey as I learned to live with the kidnapping of my seven-year-old daughter and the subsequent fifteen-month investigation of her disappearance. More importantly, it is a modern-day parable about forgiveness. As the first student of this parable, however, I often was less than receptive, and the homework required during the course was always a struggle. Were it not for the loving persistence of my Teacher, I would not have come into the truth and freedom, peace and joy I now know.

As Christians, it is absolutely essential for us to learn that forgiveness, as well as love, is a basic principle of Christianity. In the first place, it's the forgiveness which we have received in Jesus that enables us to be reconciled to God and enjoy the benefits of being His children. In the second place, forgiveness and love are the lifestyle we're called to live as children of God.

Jesus made some definite statements about the mandatory nature of forgiveness. This is what Matthew's Gospel says: "Then Peter came to Jesus and asked, 'Lord, how many times shall I forgive my brother when he sins against me? Up to seven times?' Jesus answered, 'I tell you, not seven times, but seventy-seven times'" (18:21-22).

Those are hard words! For most of us are like Peter—we

think to forgive seven times should be enough. After that, the offenders deserve what's coming to them. We want to put them down, punch them out, do them in—somehow put them as far from us as possible, and make them pay plenty!

But Jesus says, "Seventy-seven times." In other words, we must forgive them again and again, no matter how many times it takes, no matter whether they want forgiveness or not, no matter whether they know they are forgiven or not, even if they have already died. It matters not how often we pray or go to church, how we serve others, how we care for the poor—if we are not practicing forgiveness on a daily basis, we are not practicing Christians. We are not worthy of the name.

As God's children, we have received His Holy Spirit to empower us to live a Christlike life, but we often forget or choose to disregard that fact. We are caught up with the attitudes of the world, and we decide it's too much to expect of our human natures.

Fortunately, our Father knows us through and through, and knows just the right way to teach this difficult lesson. Often, life's circumstances provide the best training ground. Certainly, the extraordinary circumstances of my daughter's disappearance provided ample opportunity for the Lord to reach me and then teach me about forgiveness. By the Lord's mercy and grace, I have finally been able to receive this whole experience as "gift."

Now I share this gift with you, so that together we might say with the psalmist: "It was good for me to be afflicted so that I might learn your decrees. My comfort in my suffering is this: Your promise renews my life" (119:71, 50).

1

Journey To a Dream

My parents had been there the year before, and their hearts' desire was to get us out there, because they knew that all the things we enjoyed were plentifully present in that place. They knew if ever there was a dream vacation for us, it was camping through the "Big Sky Country" of Montana.

So they sent us tons of literature and pictures, urging over and over again that, instead of going to northern Michigan as we always had, we do something different for our next vacation, that we go to Montana. Certainly, the idea was appealing. Though a die designer by profession, my husband, Bill, was a real outdoorsman and frontier history buff, and he'd always wanted to go out West. Our five children, too, thought the idea exciting; although the teen-agers, Dan, Frank, and Heidi, typically were a little reluctant to leave their friends for any length of time. Joe, who was nine years old and an ardent nature-lover and fisherman, was eager to try his hand at catching a Loch Ness-type monster which supposedly lived in one of Montana's larger lakes. Susie, our high-spirited seven-year-old, was always ready to do something new, especially if it was something I wanted to do also.

Camping through Montana would certainly make a marvelous once-in-a-lifetime family vacation that we could talk about for years to come! As soon as it was mentioned, I, always impulsive, was ready to start packing. But Bill said, "No, it simply isn't possible." After all, he was only getting one week's paid vacation that year, and it would take more than that just for travel time out and back from our home in Michigan. If he took more time off, it would have to be without pay, and that would leave less money with which to meet expenses. Also, we'd never gone camping before as a family; we had no equipment or experience for such an adventurous undertaking. It was a great idea, but it just didn't seem feasible for us at that time.

However, our oldest son, Dan, was sixteen years old and starting to work part-time in the summer, with the others coming up right behind him. If we didn't go now as a family, we probably never would. It really seemed as if this might be the last year we would all be free to take a big summer vacation together.

Then, one early spring evening, Bill changed his mind and made the final decision. "We've said no to too many opportunities and regretted it later," he said. "This is one I won't pass by." So—yes, we would go. We would take our once-in-a-lifetime dream vacation to the magnificent state of Montana! Also, Bill decided to take extra time off from work so that we could go for a whole month. But we would have to camp in a tent, because that would be the least expensive way to travel.

Amazingly, once Bill made that decision, everything fell into place as though it was meant to be. He had no trouble getting the time off from work; moreover, we received the largest income tax refund ever, and it gave us sufficient funds for all our needs and plans. We found the kind of tent we wanted at a reasonable price, and we were able to borrow another one and some of the other necessary equipment.

As we prepared for the "great journey," we also learned as much as we could about the state of Montana. We went to the library and read about its history and people. We sent away for maps and all kinds of interesting information. In fact, by the time we started to pack all our paraphernalia, we were thinking of checking out the job and housing situation during the vacation with the hopes that we could move there permanently. Before we ever saw it, we had fallen in love with the place.

There was only one setback in my enthusiasm. My mother, in order to insure our preparedness for any eventuality, sent some magazine articles prescribing what to do when rattlesnakes or bears invaded a campsite! Her intentions were good, but I almost canceled the whole trip right then and there. It took a lot of reassurance from my husband and friends who had camped for years that the likelihood of attack by snakes or bears was indeed minimal.

We had planned to leave the day after school closed for the summer. But as camping novices are wont to do, we were taking much more than we could use, even in a month's time. So by the time we finished stowing all our gear and saying all our good-bys, it was too late in the day to start out. We decided to go to bed early and leave the next morning at dawn.

At last! The day of our departure had arrived! The little trailer we were towing was packed to the brim. We were ready and eager to begin to live our dream, (at least one of us hoping that the dream wouldn't include bears and rattlesnakes!). The seven of us piled excitedly into our van, but as Bill moved to start the engine, I said, "Wait a minute! I think we should pray first."

Though we as a family had not always been faithful to our religious duties, I had always had a faith life and a prayer life, albeit based on an improper understanding of a somewhat rigid and judgmental God who delighted in sacrifices and blind obedience. The thought had occurred to me as we were closing the house that this vacation was a significant undertaking and we needed to "officially" submit it to God.

The Lost Child

"This is not only going to be a unique and special time for us," I explained, "but also maybe the beginning of a new life in a new place. We need God's blessing." Though it was not our normal practice to pray before leaving home, everyone agreed it was appropriate to pray now, and so, together, we prayed three formal prayers.

Then, awkwardly, because I was unaccustomed to praying spontaneously, I blurted out, "Lord, we ask that You bless this vacation, give us good weather and good times, protect us from harm, keep us all safe, and show us what Your will is for us in Montana." With the family's resounding "Amen!" Bill started the engine and we were on our way!

With five children, though, our stops during the day were numerous; but our lunch stops were always fun. We were a physically active family, and we all needed to burn off a lot of energy after being confined during long periods of travel. Bill and the other kids would play ball or frisbee, while Susie and I would run around the park. When I would finally tire, she'd still want to do one more lap. I loved to sit on the grass then and watch her. Susie was tall and graceful of body for a seven-year-old and delightful to look at with her soft, wavy brown hair, expressive big, blue eyes, and pretty, happy face—so full of life! She enjoyed doing cartwheels and could do them very well, in rapid succession. So she would finish off her stint of exercise with cartwheels all over the place, while I'd set out the lunch, packed that morning at our last campsite. Then we'd all sit down and eat. Along with the banter that usually accompanied family mealtimes, we'd recount experiences-to-become-memories which we were accumulating up to that point. We were marking memories indelibly in our hearts and minds. Then after a quick cleanup, we'd board the van, ready to relax in our seats again and move on down the road through eight states to Montana.

We marveled at everything: the incredible number of out-of-state license plates around Chicago; Wisconsin's Dells; crossing the Mississippi River; the endless sky thereafter; the Badlands in South Dakota; the sparkly soil in the Black Hills; Mount Rushmore; antelope in Wyoming; and our first glorious sight of mountains!

We had good traveling weather all the way, but everywhere we stopped, people said, "It's a good thing you weren't here yesterday. We had a terrific rainstorm!" or "Yesterday there was such a strong wind, the tents were being blown down!" or "Yesterday it was much colder." I remembered how we'd left a day later than planned, and I really felt God had had His hand upon us.

The Jaegers took to camping as though we had always done it. The kids pitched right in, setting up and breaking camp like pros. It seemed we always got the best spots in the campgrounds where we spent the nights, and our knapsacks were already getting full from all the "treasures" we were collecting. This was a wonderful time of togetherness for us, exploring and enjoying a part of God's creation that we'd read about but never seen before. And we relished every moment of it!

Everything seemed in our favor. We had no car trouble. And even the few mishaps we did have were readily remedied. Once, driving along the freeway in South Dakota, Joe's glasses were accidentally whipped out the window. By the time we could slow down and pull off the road, we were a good half-mile away from where the glasses left the van. Besides the traffic on the expressway with which to contend, immediately adjacent to the pavement on both sides was a luxuriant growth of three-foot-tall grass. The possibility of finding the glasses seemed remote, let alone finding them in good condition.

For Joe, glasses were essential. I envisioned a long delay,

19

waiting in the nearest town for a few days till a new pair could be obtained; and then there was the cost to consider. But as Bill and the older kids walked back down the highway searching, there they were—sitting in the middle of the pavement, in perfect condition, never touched by any of the vehicles that had passed over them! Once again, I felt secure in God's providence and protection. In fact, by the time we crossed the Montana state line, accompanied by cheers, clapping, and whoops of delight, I was really convinced that this was where God meant us to be.

Once into Montana, our first stop was the Custer Battlefield National Monument. Having a great interest in Indian lore and western history, we thoroughly enjoyed seeing this place firsthand. Then we hurried on to our prearranged first-night-in-Montana stop at the Missouri River Headwaters Monument campground, just outside of Three Forks. My folks were waiting there for us, having come up from Arizona to share this time and be our "tour guides." It had been a long time since we'd seen each other, and we were delighted to be together again.

2

A Good-night Kiss

It had been dark when we arrived the night before, but in the morning sun, we could readily see what a wonderful spot my folks had picked for our first stop in Montana. The campground was in a lovely valley in which three rivers came together to form the Missouri River. At that time my parents were able to park their travel-trailer right alongside the Madison River, which was high and rushing because of fresh snow in the mountains surrounding the valley. As the snow melted, the rivers in the valley rose and flowed rapidly; then in a few days the waterline would recede to normal. We pitched one of our tents right next to the trailer, leaving the other packed. Our vehicles were parked immediately adjacent also, so as to form our own little compound area, though we were not isolated from the rest of the many campers, the closest being only about fifty feet away.

In our particular part of the campground, the ground was flat and grass-covered; in other places it was uneven, rocky terrain. The three rivers wound through the whole area, working to reach the point where they became the mighty Missouri. Close by, there was one high bluff which served as a lookout point; we just had to climb it before doing anything else. We were awed by that beautiful, wide-open country, with so much to see in every direction.

And of course, that's where the kids scattered—in every direction! We had to lay down some ground rules about where they could go, with whom, and when (to which, I must add, they were remarkably obedient, considering the attractions).

There were few trees in the campground area, but our site had two, which sheltered our picnic table. It was such a delight to sit there, listening to the river rushing by and gazing all around at majestic snow-capped mountains. Montana means "mountain," and I felt like I had come to rest on God's Mountain.

At that time there was a popular song called "Rocky Mountain High," and that surely was an apt description of how I felt—high! Spiritually, emotionally, and physically I was on top of the world. Surrounded by a natural beauty and grandeur my eyes had never before witnessed, I was absolutely at peace and certain we were in God's will. My husband, who had always worked such long hours to support us, was having the opportunity to really enjoy his favorite realm. Our children were getting along well and having such an enjoyable time despite the difference in ages. My folks were with us, too, after a long separation. What a blessing had been given to us with this vacation! And we still had three more weeks to celebrate! My heart was filled with elation and gratitude.

The second day at the campground we visited the Lewis and Clark Caverns and several other places nearby. Then that evening we decided to get organized and pack up again so we could move on to the next "great place" in the morning. When we had done all we could, we began to bed down for the night.

Frank, Joe, Heidi, and Susie were sleeping in our tent; Dan, our oldest, was in our van; my folks were in their trailer; and Bill and I were using my parents' camper-truck. Bill and I went into the tent to settle things down and kiss the kids good-night.

A Good-night Kiss

They were snuggled in side-by-side in their individual sleeping bags, with their heads to the back of the tent. We knelt by their feet and reached over to each one. Susie, sandwiched between Heidi and Joe, was the farthest from me. I had to lean over Heidi to reach her. Barely holding her, my lips just skimmed across Susie's cheek as I tried to kiss her.

"Oh, no, Mama," she exclaimed, "not like that!" And she pulled herself out of her sleeping bag, climbed over her sister, and got right in front of me. She wrapped her arms around my neck and gave me a great big kiss on my mouth. "There, Mama," said my precious youngest child, "that's the way it should be!" and happily snuggled back down into her sleeping bag.

I treasure that moment, and every time I remember it, I am filled with such gratitude to my Lord for inspiring it. It was so like the loving Father I now know He is to give me that last, precious memory.

3

Please Send the Sun

Around five o'clock in the morning, while it was still dark, our thirteen-year-old daughter, Heidi woke up and felt a breeze on the back of her head. Thinking that perhaps the back of the tent had collapsed and that the breeze was coming through the tent window which would now be at ground level, she reached behind her head with her arm. Surprised to feel grass, she came fully awake and, sitting up, realized that there was a hole in the back of the tent. And Susie was gone!

With a sense of foreboding, Heidi ran to wake us. "There's a big hole in the tent and I can't find Susie!" she cried.

Bill was immediately out of bed and running to the tent with Heidi. In an instant he was back. "It's true!" he exclaimed, grabbing flashlights and pulling me to my feet and out the door of the camper. "Susie's gone!"

"Dan, quick! Wake up! It's an emergency!" we called to our oldest son as we ran past the van.

All the commotion woke fourteen-year-old Frank and he joined us, but Joe had burrowed down to the closed end of his sleeping bag and was oblivious to everything. Because he was so young, we chose not to wake him, but I went into my folk's trailer to rouse them.

I had to stop and think—although they were healthy, active, younger-than-most retirees, I didn't know what to say that would wake them but not unduly frighten them.

The Lost Child

Yet, I was anxious for them to help look for Susie, as Bill and our older children already were. I gently shook my mother's hand and spoke in as calm a voice as I could muster, "Mom, please don't be upset, but Susie's gone and we need you and dad to help look for her." In short order, they were both dressed and outside with their flashlights, joining the search.

We questioned Heidi carefully. Could she remember any sound, anyone's presence, anything, as she woke up? "I only know that Susie was there around 1:30," she sobbed, "because we both woke up and talked for a little bit. We were thinking about going into grandma and grandpa's trailer, but we decided not to because they would probably wake up and we didn't want to bother them. So we decided to stay there in the tent. Then we went back to sleep and when I woke up again, Susie was gone and there was a hole in the tent!" She was so sorry she had nothing else to remember.

Trying to pursue every possible explanation, we asked the other children, "Was there anything in the tent that Susie could have used to cut the hole herself—a pair of scissors or a jackknife?" But no, there had been nothing—only the children and their sleeping bags. All clothing, supplies, and equipment that were not still in our trailer were in the screened-in front area of the tent, separated from the sleeping area by a canvas partition that was still zippered and tied shut when Heidi awoke and discovered Susie missing.

I don't think I shall ever be able to put into words the fear and terror that began to well up inside the deepest part of me as I became fully awake and alert and the realization of what might have happened to my little girl began to take hold of me. As I stumbled around the campground searching, I was gripped by a terrible sense of separation, panic, and hopelessness in my inability to see. I remember looking up at the black night sky and begging God to send the sun; the darkness was unbearably frustrating. All our efforts seemed so futile, but we could not just stand still. "O God," I prayed desperately, "please help us!"

We looked everywhere. Behind bushes. Around buildings and campsites. We even woke other campers. But Susie was nowhere to be found. We discovered that at the back of the tent, near the floor, an opening had been cut just behind where Susie's head had been. Someone had apparently reached in, pulled her out, and taken her away! Outside the hole, on the grass, we found the stuffed animals Susie had been holding in her arms when she went to sleep. Other than that, there was no sign of Susie anywhere. Soon, some early-rising campers began preparing to leave. My dad planted himself in the middle of the road leading out of the campground so that no one could depart without being checked.

As it became apparent that Susie was not in the immediate area, Bill and dad jumped into the van and drove to the nearest town to get the police. They found the town marshall, and before he left his office to come to the park, he notified both the Sheriff's Department and the F.B.I. Within a short time, the campground was swarming with law enforcement people.

All vehicles and all buildings on the premises were searched; all campers were wakened and questioned. All the men, law enforcement and volunteer searchers, formed a long, straight line, an arm's length apart; and stooping close to the ground, this line of men moved slowly over the campground, scouring the grass for any possible clue.

Bill and dad joined the searchers, while Mom and I stayed at the campsite with the children. As we stood there, giving information to the sheriff, I watched while investigators carefully examined the tent. Suddenly I remembered Joey, still sleeping in the bottom of his sleeping bag! Knowing he would be terrified if he woke up with strange men standing over him, I asked the men to back off for a moment. Reaching down into his bag, I pulled Joe out and woke him. Leading him over to the trailer, I explained as best I could what had happened, why all this activity and all these strangers were in our camp. Susie was Joey's best friend in all the world, and as soon as he was able to grasp my words, he hurried to dress so he could search too.

One thing we overheard right away in the conversation of the searchers was that a young boy sleeping in a tent in this same campground had been stabbed to death a few years previously. When we asked the officials about this, they verified the statement. However, there seemed to be so much confusion as to exactly what had happened in that particular situation that Bill and I wondered how they could ever be able to determine any connection with Susie's disappearance.

The F.B.I. took charge as soon as they arrived, setting up a trailer and telephone on the grounds as their headquarters. From there they supervised the continuing search, the questioning of suspects, and the investigation of all leads and information.

The portion of the tent where the cut had been made, Susie's stuffed animals, and her sleeping bag were sent to a lab for further study. The Sheriff's Department conducted a house-to-house search of all homes and buildings for miles around. Search-and-rescue squads who were trained to find people lost in the wilderness were brought in. Some businesses closed down for a day so that their employees could join the search. One group spent a whole day working in the hot sun, sifting through tons of smelly garbage and putrid animal corpses at the local dump. My dad was one of the men who took on this horribly distasteful, but necessary, job. I protested, not wanting him to go through this ordeal, but dad insisted, "If Susie's found in that terrible place, I want to be there for her."

Boy Scouts searched through thick underbrush with machetes. Men rode up into the hills on horseback and motorcycles and four-wheel-drive vehicles. Farmers and ranchers checked out every nook and cranny of their lands. Owners of tracking dogs came in to help. Pilots volunteered their time and planes to fly over the open country. Men searched up and down the rivers in boats. Still, long day after long day, there was no sign of Susie. No sign of her any-where. All we could do was wait and try to bolster each other's hope and courage.

Some suspects began turning up, mostly men who were loners or of a questionable past or behavior. Those who could not verify their whereabouts during the early morning hours of June 25, 1973, were required to take a polygraph exam.

Leads began to come from all over the state. Since Mon-tana borders Canada, the Canadian Royal Mounted Police were also put on the alert. I especially remember one tip which said that a child resembling Susie had been seen at a highway rest stop with a man in a blue Volkswagen. The "child" later was determined to be a small young woman, but before that happened, every blue Volkswagen traveling across Montana was stopped a half dozen times to be searched thoroughly. Even some private citizens, so distressed that a child could be taken like that in their midst, took it upon themselves to stop and search vehicles in the hopes that they might find Susie. One poor man, who meant well, made the mistake of holding someone at gunpoint with a shotgun while he searched the car and ended up spending the night in jail himself for overzealous vigilante action.

Occasionally one of the searchers would find an article of clothing, such as socks or underwear, which would then be brought back to us for identification. This was always difficult, both for us and for the person who had to show it to us, but nothing that was found belonged to Susie. She seemed to have utterly vanished from this earth without trace.

Meanwhile, back in Michigan, our house was being checked and our mail inspected for any contact by the kidnapper. All our neighbors, relatives, and friends were questioned. Did they know anything that might be pertinent to the investigation? Did they know anyone who had a grudge against us, anyone who would want to hurt us, anyone who had followed us out to Montana? Did we have any enemies they knew about?

We ourselves racked our brains. Did we know anyone who wanted to hurt us, anyone who would want Susie for themselves? Who could have done such a horrible thing? Where was she? How was she? And the hardest question of all—will we ever get her back?

"Please, God, let her be alive and well," was my daily prayer.

4

God's Good People

From the day Susie was taken, they began to come to us—
the people of Montana. They came from nearby towns and
the farthest parts of the state; and if they couldn't personally
visit us, they wrote letters. It was as if, in some way, they felt
responsible to compensate to us, as much as possible, for this
terrible thing that had happened in their beloved Montana. In
the best Christian sense, they formed a sort of community
around us, caring for and serving us in any and every way
they could.

They fed us with vegetables from their land, milk and
meat from their cattle, bread, cookies, and cakes from their
ovens. They regularly sent whole meals, cooked and ready to
be eaten. People who owned stores sent bags of groceries.
During the whole month we stayed there, we did not have to
buy any food!

The Montanans brought books, puzzles, and games for
the children. They brought their children to play with ours.
They took them swimming, to the movies, took them to
their homes, ranches, and farms so our kids could see what
life was like there and participate in it.

A group of archaeological students were camped near
us, working in a cave nearby, and they took our children to
see their findings. Another group of college students, having
studied the travels of Lewis and Clark, were now reliving
them by means of raft trips down the rivers; they came to

take our children and my mother to share in the experience with them. When the rodeo came to town, we were given free tickets, and some of the cowboys came to visit and tell us tales of their lifestyle. A traveling group of young Christian people gave an impromptu concert for us in the campground.

One young man, who came often, taught us about the history of the area and gave us treasured souvenirs of obsidian rock and petrified wood found on his father's ranch. The town doctor came and offered his services should we need them. Catholic priests and ministers from many Christian denominations shared their faith and encouraged us. Quite a few of the law enforcement people working on the case would bring their families to visit on their off-duty hours.

We received an incredible amount of mail, most of which had money enclosed to help with any expenses. Every need we expressed was met as quickly as possible. And these dear people thought of many things we didn't mention or even think of ourselves!

From the very beginning, there were also many media people, television crews and newspaper reporters, who spent time with us, most from the West or from Michigan. They were there to do a job, but many extended themselves in a personal way—playing games with the kids, obtaining information for us, setting up reward funds and opportunities for the kidnapper to make contact through the newspapers. And just waiting with us.

The people of Montana came to see us by the hundreds, some from many miles away. What a lesson they taught me about caring and sharing and unhesitatingly reaching out to those in need. Some came often and became our good friends. They spent hour after hour, day after day with us, helping to pass the time as we waited for each new development in the case. Each night before they left, we'd gather in a big circle and pray together—a kind of spontaneous prayer that I'd never experienced previously. I came from a background of formal prayer, so this was brand-new to me. I loved the closeness it presumed of God and the way we could really speak of our specific needs: "Father, we ask You to intervene in Susie's disappearance, to guide those in charge of the investigation, to touch the heart of her kidnapper, and to grant us strength and courage until You bring Susie back to us." How I came to treasure this time of prayer with our wonderful new friends!

We shared hours and hours of delightful, interesting, and enlightening conversations with these good Christian people. Though we never got to see much of Montana, we certainly learned much more about the people and their lifestyles than we ever would have had our vacation progressed as originally planned.

I often wondered, though, how some people felt as they drove up to see us, to offer sympathy, only to find us sitting around the picnic table laughing and talking, or playing frisbee on the lawn. I'm sure it must have seemed incongruous, or even in bad taste. But it had much to do with keeping ourselves from drowning in despair and terror. I really learned how very important it is, in that kind of dire situation, to maintain one's equilibrium and perspective. I needed to laugh as well as cry; I needed to talk of other things. Because I could never escape the inner and keen awareness of Susie's disappearance and the anguish that constantly threatened to engulf me, I found it essential to allow myself to be distracted or occupied as much as possible. Even though I was trying to trust God, my natural inclination was to isolate myself and give in to my grief. But to do that would have surely broken me completely.

Scripture says: "You can trust God not to let you be tried beyond your strength, and with any trial He will give you a way out of it and the strength to bear it" (1 Cor. 10:13

33

JB). Those good people of Montana were my "way out of it." Their ongoing presence at our campsite was the distraction and diversion I needed to survive.

If ever I saw the value of Christian community, it was there in that place. Truly God loved and cared for us in a special way through the willing and wonderful people of Montana. How we needed them to help us pass the interminable days as we waited for word of our little girl.

5

A Ravaged Heart

About one week after Susie was kidnapped, just before we were ready to go to bed, the sheriff's deputy who was manning the F.B.I. trailer overnight came to the door of my folk's trailer and called Bill outside.

"I just received a call from my wife," he said to Bill, "and she says a man just called our house in town and said that he has Susie." The man had stated that he wanted fifty thousand dollars in ransom and that the money was to be put in a locker in a bus station in Denver, Colorado. "In case you don't believe me," the caller had added, "I can tell you that the little girl has humpy fingernails." In order to determine if this was an authentic demand and not just another crank call, the deputy wanted to know, "Does this term, 'humpy fingernails,' mean anything to you?"

As Bill reentered the trailer and approached me, I stood up, struck by the intense expression on his face. He repeated the deputy's words. I remember falling to my knees as my husband reached out to catch me in his arms. My mind was spinning, my legs weak. How could we have forgotten?

When Susie was born, I had had no anesthesia and was fully awake and aware as the doctor laid her across my chest. As I inspected my new daughter, the first thing I noticed was that the fingernails on both her index fingers were deformed. The fingers themselves were perfect, but the nails were thickened and rounded rather than flat against her fingers; they were "humpy." I remembered asking, "God, why have You allowed such a minor deformity, when none of my other children have any at all?" Surely, because she was a girl, she'd want pretty hands. Why had He allowed it to happen? Then, I remembered the serious deformities with which some children are born, and I thanked God for this child and declared, "I accept her just as You have given her to me."

After that, as Susie was growing up, we rarely even noticed those fingernails; that is, until just the year before we came to Montana. She had started school that year, and her classmates had noticed them. They would question her about them and sometimes tease her, as little ones are inclined to do. Susie would come home upset, and we'd have to sit down and talk about it until she felt better about herself.

But when Susie was taken and we had to give the F.B.I. a complete description, we had remembered every mark, scar, scratch, and bruise from her head to her toes, everything *except* her two deformed fingernails. Somehow it was completely blocked from all our memories. So that when this man called and identified her by them, we knew it was an authentic call. Only someone who had seen her would know about those fingernails! It couldn't even have been leaked information from official confidential documents, because it was never recorded. From now on, though, it became a closely guarded secret—our only means of identifying the real kidnapper.

Now, too, I knew in the deepest part of me why God had allowed those fingernails to be deformed; it was for this circumstance that she'd been marked in the womb. Though I still didn't know what was happening or why, it was reassuring that somehow God had prepared Susie and His hand was still working in the midst of this nightmare. Maybe now He would bring her back to us! At the very least, we knew for certain there was a real kidnapper, and he had finally made contact with us.

On the advice of the F.B.I., who had been notified immediately by the deputy, my husband took a middle-of-the-night ride into town to use a public phone, as if to make an attempt to raise money to meet the kidnapper's demand. This was done in case the man was watching so that he would think we were trying to move as he desired. None of us slept that night, waiting and hoping that the kidnapper would call again. But morning came and still no word, still no Susie.

It was presumed that the kidnapper had called this particular deputy's home because the local newspaper had recently mentioned that he was a frequent visitor to our campsite. Although the arrangements for the ransom exchange were incomplete and couldn't be acted upon without further communication from the kidnapper, we knew it would be best if we had the fifty thousand dollars ready and waiting. However, knowing it and having it were two different stories. We certainly didn't have that kind of money, nor did we know anyone else who did. Even if we could find some way to borrow it, we didn't know how we'd ever be able to pay it back. We didn't know where to go, where to turn, how to get that much money together quickly with any kind of a guarantee that we'd ever be able to repay. Yet, it was our only chance of having Susie returned to us. We had to have that fifty thousand dollars!

My folks, in the meantime, had been making some phone calls of their own. One of their dear friends knew of a slight possibility, but needed time to check it out. We waited, apprehensive that the kidnapper would call again before we had the money, and yet so eager for a word of Susie. Finally, the friend returned my parents' call. Fifty thousand dollars had been made available to us; an unknown man, desiring to remain anonymous, would deposit the needed money in a special bank account! Now we were ready to negotiate.

Days went by and still no call came from the kidnapper with the final details for the exchange. Of course, I knew that the first call could have just been a ploy to throw us off the track and that Susie might not even be alive. At this time, very consciously, I chose to believe she was still alive, until such time, if ever, that I would have to accept positive proof to the contrary.

It was difficult to maintain that stance. If Susie was still alive, where was she? Was she being cared for, fed, kept warm? Was she suffering, frightened, terrorized? What did she have to endure? Then—there were those questions I couldn't even bring myself to put into mental words.

Finally, I could not bear one more agonizing minute. The search-and-rescue squads kept coming back empty-handed; the search planes droned overhead. Original suspects were being released because of insufficient evidence or their passing of the lie detector tests. The authorities seemed to be running out of leads to investigate. The police boats were dragging the river alongside us, and every time they stopped, my heart stopped too—I was terrified that they'd find her body in the water! I kept finding the other children off by themselves, crying, not wanting to upset the rest of us. We were all trying to stay strong for each other. I could not bear to look into Bill's eyes one more time and see the anguish there.

That night I lay beside him, my whole being raging furiously at being so at the mercy of the merciless kidnapper. Finally, I said aloud and deliberately, "Even if he were to bring Susie back this moment, alive and well, I could kill him for what he has done to my family!" and I meant it with every fiber of my being. I wanted this horrible person to experience the kind of suffering he had inflicted upon us. I wanted him to pay for every moment of anguish we had had to endure.

But no sooner had I uttered those words than a voice within me said, *But that's not how I want you to feel.*

"I know Christians are called to forgive their enemies, Lord, but this is different! This is my daughter. It's only normal and natural for me to feel this way. It's only normal and natural to want to avenge my little girl. It's only right and just to desire punishment for this man. I have the right to seek revenge, and I want to make sure I get it. I want justice done!" Oh, how I wrestled with the Lord. How I argued my case.

But God said very clearly, *Vengeance is mine.* I knew He was calling me to let go of all my hateful feelings, to be willing to forgive the kidnapper. God wanted me to let Him be Lord of the situation, to give up my rights. Still I argued and struggled. But God is persistent. He wouldn't let me go until I was willing to let go of all those ugly feelings that He knew would only destroy me in the end.

Finally, by His Grace, which is always there, I gave in; I surrendered. I knew, though, that I had to be honest. "Just because I am willing to forgive the man and act accordingly doesn't mean I actually have those feelings for him. In fact, I can't imagine how I ever could. But if that's how You want me to feel, then You will have to make it happen."

So, before my resolve could weaken, I made three requests of the Lord: "Please enable me not only to forgive this man with my lips, but to love him with my heart." (I figured if I was going to do it, I might as well go all the way.) "Please let me be involved with the resolution, whenever it is." (So much time had elapsed that we would soon have to return to Michigan, and I felt that I would be so far from the investigation, so far from Susie.) And finally, "Please, God, if something terrible has happened to Susie, help me to understand why." (I knew that sometimes kidnapped children did suffer horrible deaths; but we had asked God's blessing and protection, and it had almost seemed that He was drawing us out to Montana. If God had allowed anything terrible to happen to Susie, it just didn't seem fair that I should have to accept it in blind obedience and faith.) But again, I made a conscious decision to believe that Susie was alive.

With that prayer, peace came into my heart. For the first time since Susie's disappearance, I slept well all night.

6

A Family in Waiting

Late one afternoon, we heard a commotion outside. A helicopter was landing across the road. From the excitement generated by the people running toward it, I thought that Susie had been found—"They've brought her back to us in a helicopter!" I raced over, my heart pounding! I felt like I was going to burst with joy!

As I reached the landing place, I saw that only two people had stepped out, the pilot remaining inside. Suddenly the truth of the situation hit me: they were not bringing Susie back to us; they were only dropping other people off. Recoiling in abject disappointment, I stumbled back down the hill, my joyous exhilaration shattered into nothingness, hardly able to see for the tears in my eyes. Now it seemed I could not bear the pain; I just wanted to die.

I ran back to my parents' trailer, seeking only to hide, to be alone in my grief. But soon my mother followed and called me back outside. Understanding how I felt, she gently explained who the people were who had come to our campground by helicopter. It seems I had turned my back and fled from the governor of Montana and his wife, who had stopped for no other reason than to visit us, express their concern, and offer any help available through the government. I apologized for my seemingly ungracious welcome, but they understood and were not at all offended. Their warmth and kindness and personal visit meant a great deal to us.

The Lost Child

After about three weeks, the F.B.I. moved the center of the investigation from the trailer in the campground back to their offices in Bozeman, a large city not too far away. The removal of their trailer from our midst left us feeling insecure and fearful. We felt vulnerable now that there was no official sign of their presence in the campground. We became suspicious of every car that drove by and every unknown face we saw. However, these fears soon dissipated as the agents regularly stopped by to visit, check on our welfare, and inform us of any new developments.

No bears or rattlesnakes ever did invade our campsite, although we did see rattlers in the area. The only bothersome wildlife were the mosquitoes; they almost carried us off each evening after the sun went down.

Bill and the kids kept us supplied with freshly caught trout, for we were surrounded by world-famous fishing rivers. We went for many exploratory walks and rides through the hills surrounding the campground. Remarkably, considering the horrifying situation in which we were immersed, the Lord kept our eyes clear enough to see and enjoy the natural beauty of His creation.

One evening at dusk, Bill and I were moving slowly along in our van when, suddenly, two large horses galloped along the crest of a hill right in front of us, their manes and tails flared out behind them, their dark bodies magnificently silhouetted against the backdrop of a blazing gold, crimson, and purple sunset. We were awestruck at the beauty of the sight. People pay thousands of dollars to own paintings of just such scenes; we were privileged to see the real thing, captured forever in our memories—a gift from God to lift our heavily burdened hearts.

One of God's special means of providence for me was my mother's company there in Montana. Not only were her faith and strength a beacon for me, and her love and understanding such a comfort and support, but the Lord wisely saw that we complemented each other in very practical terms. When I am in an exceedingly tense situation, I can be with people and carry on a conversation with reasonable ease, but I find it difficult to accomplish my chores. I just can't seem to focus my mind on any job that needs to be done. My mother, on the other hand, finds it helpful to her state of mind, in that kind of situation, to keep busy. She becomes task-oriented. There in Montana, on any given day, there were apt to be many different people milling around—law enforcement, media, and/or townsfolk—and I was often needed "out front," to talk with them. Had it been up to me, there may never have been a pot of coffee made or a meal prepared. But there was my mother, serving in the background, doing all those chores that needed to be done every day to keep order. She kept the coffee coming and the meals on the table, the trailer neat and clean. I can't imagine how I would have handled those things had she not been there; but, as in every instance of this incredible situation, the Lord had it covered, and specifically so with the gift of my mother's presence.

My dad, too, was always there working behind the scenes, maintaining the physical environment in which all eight of us were living. As much as possible, he remained involved in the searches, staying strong and supportive even as his heart ached for fear of what had happened to his beloved little granddaughter.

My husband's heroic courage was a great support for me also. Bill is not the kind of man to walk around wringing his hands, bemoaning fate. His quiet strength and his ability to exercise common sense and function with normalcy in an abnormal situation were a real anchor for me. An accomplished outdoorsman, there was much he was able to teach our children about their surroundings. Together, all of us tried to use every opportunity to see and draw good from this period when evil had invaded our lives with such magnitude.

Through God's grace, Bill and I were both enabled to properly care for Dan, Frank, Joe, and Heidi with some degree of wisdom and understanding during this traumatic time. Amazingly, we did not react to Susie's disappearance by being overly protective of the rest. It was as if we felt the worst had happened and no more misfortune would befall us; although neither were we so caught up with the investigation or our own personal anguish that we allowed them to go their way with reckless abandon.

And the children—it is difficult to describe how well they seemed to handle this tragedy in their lives. I suppose the fact that they were in a new and fascinating place, surrounded by good and friendly people, helped a great deal. I think also the fact that Bill and I and my parents were able to remain generally composed enabled the children to set a similar tone to their demeanor.

In retrospect, I know that what started as pride in my own self-control soon became an occasion of gratitude for God's faithfulness in my weakness. For as I write this, remembering, I can't imagine being able to survive that time on my own strength. I'm certain it was by His grace that I remained fully aware and in control of my behavior—and capable of coping without the use of drugs or alcohol. I mention the latter only because I was surprised at how often drugs or alcohol were suggested to me as an aid under the circumstances. I'm so grateful that I did not give in to the strong and understandable desire to escape, even temporarily, the horrible reality of those first days. To have done so would have been to miss the opportunity to fully experience the sufficiency of God's grace.

I hasten to add, however, that none of us lost touch with our humanity. The children were normally rambunctious and we adults were normally limited in patience. One night at bedtime I became so exasperated at one son's lack of co-operation that I really lost my temper. I'm embarrassed to admit that the whole campground must have heard me! But it sure got rid of a lot of tension, and of course, there were apologies all around later.

My biggest problem was believing that Susie had really been kidnapped. This sort of thing happened to other people, not to us. I kept wanting to shake my head, wake up, and find it was only a nightmare. But as the reality was inescapable, so was God's grace sufficient to endure it.

And thus it went, day after day, until the time came for us to leave Montana. I was tormented by the fear that as we were closing up our tent, the F.B.I. was closing its file on Susie. I knew that wasn't true. But I had to struggle to believe it. It seemed as if once we left Montana, we were leaving Susie forever. The truth was that there would be an F.B.I. agent waiting for us back in Michigan, and we would be only a phone call away from anything that developed. So much time had elapsed that Susie could have been taken anywhere in the country, and for all anyone knew, we might even be closer to her in Michigan. As difficult as it was to leave Montana, I had to acknowledge that it was easier to leave with hope than without.

As we packed everything away that last day, the sky became dark and threatening. For the whole four weeks we had been in the campground, there had been sunshine every day. Gratefully, I had seen it as another sign of God's providence for us, as we needed to depend on the outdoors for living space. More personally, I had gratefully seen it as a sign of God's providence for me. Weather greatly affects my feelings and mood, and I believed He had purposely kept away the gray, dreary skies so I could be strong and properly care for my family. But now on this last day it was going to rain, and it seemed an appropriate setting. My heart was so heavy; how long could we keep on living like this? What was happening to Susie? Would we ever get her back? Would I ever hold my little girl again?

At the last moment, as the sun was setting, the rain stopped. The clouds blew away, and there, splashed across that huge Montana sky, was a gorgeous double rainbow! As I looked at it in awe, I saw it as God's promise that He was still with us, working in this and watching over Susie. He would not forsake her or us. Now I could leave in peace. Now I could go home.

7

A Zinnia for Hope

Before we were even out of Montana, our van developed engine trouble. We were following my folks, who were driving their truck towing their trailer, and very soon were unable to keep up with them. The engine was backfiring loudly and the van was barely able to move. "Oh, God," I prayed, "it was so difficult to leave that campground. Please help us to keep moving now that we've started." But the trouble got worse, and it seemed we'd never get to the next town where there might be a garage.

I marveled at Bill's control and composure. Our emotions had been so raw and spilling over when we circled the campground for the last time as we departed. I knew Bill didn't need this aggravation at all, but he remained calm and steady at the wheel as we inched along up the hills.

Finally, a town came into view, along with my folks waiting at the exit ramp for us to catch up. About this time I was wondering where God was. But we found Him too, waiting at a service station which just happened to specialize in our particular make of van, right by the expressway. There, they recognized our name from all the publicity, rapidly replaced the defective part at reduced cost, and sent us on our way.

The children traveled well, as they had the first time, but all of us were much more subdued. The enthusiasm and eager anticipation that had filled the atmosphere on our trip out to

The Lost Child

Montana was replaced by minimal interest in passing scenery and dogged determination to get home as quickly as possible.

Though we were not inhibited in mentioning Susie, conversation did not come easily; everything seemed so unsettled, so unfinished. It was as if no one wanted to talk until there was something definite and positive to say. When we did speak, most of our sentences seemed to start with, "When . . ." or "If . . . ." A member of our family, a part of us, had been torn away, and we had had to leave the last place we'd all been together; the pain of our anguished incompleteness was expressed in our uncommon quietness and reluctance to engage in normal family chatter.

I was constantly reminded of Susie's absence. On our way to Montana, I had picked up the habit of counting heads to make certain everyone was in the van whenever we were ready to move on. I found myself doing it again on the way home, only to be jolted repeatedly with the fact that we were returning with four children, not five. Our return trip took only four days, but it seemed much longer than that. The F.B.I. had been given our travel route and probable night stops in case they needed to contact us, but I couldn't wait to get home and next to the phone.

Of course, our greatest hope was that the kidnapper would contact us again. As soon as we got home, Bill bought a tape recorder with a special attachment for the phone so we could record every call received concerning Susie's disappearance.

We decided that either Bill or I would stay at home at all times in case an important call did come. Consequently, as he had to go to work, I did little else but "sit on the phone," waiting. Because of the nationwide publicity, besides a volume of mail, we received hundreds of calls. Some offered prayers and encouragement; some suggested a person or situation that should be investigated. Many people called collect from far away, but we felt we had to accept all calls, just in case one was "the one" for which we were waiting. As a result of this along with our calls to Montana, our monthly phone bill regularly equaled our house payment.

Soon after our return, an extortion attempt was made over the phone, and the man was arrested by the F.B.I. while he was still conversing with my husband. There were also some crank calls, and callers who would hang up after we answered. Each time this happened, I wondered if it was the kidnapper. We never knew what to expect when the phone rang, but we all soon learned to start the tape recorder before we picked up the receiver.

Before we left for Montana, we had planted flower and vegetable gardens. When I finally got around to checking the yard, I could see that most of the plants had died. The weather in Michigan had been either too dry or too wet while we'd been gone, and everything had withered. But as I checked the flower bed by our front porch, I spotted something that made my heart stand still.

For Mother's Day, Susie had given me a tiny zinnia seedling she had started herself in school from seed. Together, we had carefully planted it in the flower bed. Now, amid all the dried-up plants, there was a huge, gorgeous, bright red zinnia, alive and thriving! It was a sign to me of my little girl's love—a love no one could ever change or take away, a love that was precious beyond words, a love that would be forever mine. I thought of how extravagantly Susie loved. She could never pass me by without stopping to give me a hug and a kiss. How I delighted in her unabashed love. Now here was this large, flashy flower, an appropriate symbol and reminder of my little girl's lavish affection for me. Could this also be a sign that Susie was still alive? I wondered. If only the kidnapper would call again.

In order to try to generate more leads and because the

kidnapper had designated a place in another western state for the ransom exchange when he had called the deputy sheriff's home, we decided to write to the governors of all the states and request that specific publicity be given to Susie's abduction. Sufficient time had elapsed that she could have been taken anywhere in the country.

In the letter we stated:

> We feel that our best hope lies in keeping the case in front of the public, to insure their interest in every child of Susie's general description. However, we are at the mercy of newspaper editors and television station managers. Although the information concerning Susie has long been available on teletype, many medias do not consider it sufficiently newsworthy for their area.

> If you could use the prestige of your high office to stimulate public interest in your state, it could be just the push needed to resolve this case.

We also asked them to release to the media an enclosed letter to the kidnapper, imploring him to call again as we were ready with the ransom.

Amazingly, since it was a rather presumptuous request, we received personal replies from all the governors except one, and each indicated his desire to help. Some called to speak with us personally; many sent newspaper clippings to show that they had complied. It was truly heartwarming to receive such generous response from busy, important people who may well have doubted that anything of value would turn up in their part of the country.

Some new leads did come in through this effort. Also, people who considered themselves psychic picked up the information from the media and began calling with their premonitions and visions. We did not expect the case to be resolved in this manner, but we did learn that it had been the experience of law enforcement agencies that a criminal whose conscience is beginning to bother him will sometimes seek out a well-known psychic through whom to divulge factual information regarding the whereabouts of the victim. Thus the case is solved, the criminal goes free, and the psychic gets the credit. So every time a "psychic" lead came in, the F.B.I. would have to check it out carefully, no matter how unlikely it seemed.

In September, three months after Susie had been taken, one such lead came in through a phone call to me. The description of the location—a canyon in a national forest in southeastern Montana—where Susie supposedly could be found was so graphic that it seemed to be an authentic lead.

According to this "vision," experienced by a psychic friend of the caller, "Your daughter's in a riverbed and it's dry right now, but there's been rain and the water's comin' down from the mountains and it's gonna fill up fast. You gotta get her out of there!" He described precisely the appearance of the canyon, the location of trees and bluffs.

"How did Susie get there?" I asked. "Is she hurt?"

"A large, dark blue car drove up near that place—had a Montana license plate—and someone just shoved your little girl out the door."

"Was she hurt?" I asked again.

"She didn't move at first, but then she got up and started wandering around like she was in a daze. But she's been there a couple of days now and she hasn't had anything to eat so she's really weak. She fell into the riverbed earlier today and can't climb out. She'll drown soon if you don't find her quick!"

As soon as we got this information to the F.B.I., they began an intense search of the forest area described to me. Ranchers and farmers came out to help. Helicopters searched from the skies. We sat by the phone, anxiously awaiting word. After many hours of scouring the area, it was determined that Susie was not there. Once again, we had to swallow our disappointment, calm our pounding hearts, and go on with our vigil.

Several days later, my youngest son called from his catechism class. "Mom, the lady who brings me home didn't come today, and it's raining hard outside. Can you come and get me?" he asked. Bill was not home to man the phone, but Joe was only five minutes away. I could pick him up and be back in a jiffy. Also, I reasoned, the kidnapper had not called in the three months we'd been home; certainly he wouldn't call during the brief time I'd be gone. So I dashed out to get Joe.

As I walked into the house a short time later, Dan had just hung up the phone and turned off the tape recorder. The kidnapper had called!

He had identified Susie by her "humpy fingernails," said that she was well and that he still wanted to exchange her for ransom. His problem was determining a way to collect the money and yet not get caught. "Don't worry—I'll call again," he had said, and that was the end of the conversation.

The F.B.I. was able to trace the call. The kidnapper had placed the call through the operator, charging it to someone who had the same last name as ours. He had used the phone in a diner in a small town in Wyoming, just south of the national forest area which had been searched so thoroughly a few days previously because of the psychic's vision. We presumed the publicity of that search had provoked the kidnapper to call. Once again, we had nothing to move on. But still, somewhere out West, there was someone who knew where Susie was!

During all the time since Susie had been taken, her godparents, our closest friends, had been standing by, sharing our pain, and wanting to help, but not knowing what to do.

Now, as a result of this latest development, they presented a new course of action: Perhaps the kidnapper had confided in someone; or perhaps for some other reason someone was aware of the kidnapper's identity; if so, this person might be enticed to bring forth the information in exchange for a sizeable reward, much more than had been offered by the newspapers. (While we were still out west, a large daily paper in Detroit, Michigan, had offered $2000 in reward money for information about Susie, and a Bozeman, Montana, paper had also offered a comparable amount.)

None of us had that kind of money, but since Susie's disappearance had generated such an abundance of publicity and such sympathetic response, perhaps the general public would be willing to contribute to a reward fund. Even if individual donations were minimal, if a sufficient number of persons responded it would be possible to accumulate a large amount of money. If the reward went unclaimed, all money would be returned to the donors. Susie's godparents offered to take complete charge of the venture, assisted by a high school classmate of mine, now an attorney, who would give legal counsel to insure absolute propriety.

After the legally required corporation was organized, with the kind cooperation of the governor of Michigan, all media people of the metropolitan area of Detroit, Michigan, were invited to a press conference. It had been decided that I would make the presentation and request. The problem would be to convince people that a reward offer was justified without divulging the fact that the kidnapper had called again. We did not want to jeopardize any further attempts he might make to contact us, so I had to convey the fact that we had valid hope without being able to explain why. It was humbling to ask strangers for money, but desperation gave me the courage to speak.

After the press conference, all we could hope for was

that the media would consider it sufficiently newsworthy to publicize, and if they did, that the public would respond to my plea. Anxiously, we awaited the results.

Within just a few days, the mail started pouring in. Senior citizens on retirement incomes sent one, two, or five dollars each. Children sent in their allowances. Businesses sent large checks. Individuals and families took up collections. Charitable organizations set aside funds for our cause. Relatives and friends gave generously, as did my church. There were many anonymous donations, as well as hundreds of compassionate personal letters accompanying checks. Stores in our area set up collection containers on their counters; teen-agers went door-to-door asking people to contribute. Susie's school had a used book sale, with profits going to the reward fund. The Jaycees had a Christmas tree sale. Montanans and people from other states sent money also. Susie's plight had touched many hearts, and people responded with incredible generosity.

My attorney friend set up a temporary office where Susie's godmother, my sister-in-law, aunt, and friends could carry out the work involved. Many hours and much effort were spent by this team of volunteers. As the money came in, exact records were kept; every cent was recorded and deposited into a special bank account. All expenditures involved were generously paid for out of the pockets of the people working on the project.

Finally, the day came when they had to stop collecting money and move ahead to the next step. A dear and longtime friend was a printer, and he provided, at his own expense, ten thousand posters advertising a reward of fourteen thousand dollars for information leading to the safe return of Susie. The volunteer team assembled again, this time to prepare for mailing a package of posters to *each* sheriff's office of *each* county in Montana and *all* of the surrounding states. Enclosed in each package was a letter explaining what we were trying to accomplish with this effort and asking for their cooperation in the distribution of the posters, possibly by obtaining the aid of local Boy Scouts or service organizations. We told them that our aim was to keep Susie's name and face in the public's view and to entice anyone with information to call us.

Once the packages were prepared for mailing, Susie's godmother hauled them in her car to the post office at the end of the day. The postmaster came out to help her cart them in to be weighed. She expected the total mailing cost to be in excess of one hundred dollars and was prepared to pay that amount out of her own money. But the postmaster told her that since it was late, the postal employees on the next shift would weigh and process the bundles and she could come the next day to pay the required fees. Early the next morning, the postmaster called my friend to say all was in readiness and asked her to please stop in his office when she came.

When Susie's godmother arrived at the post office to pay the postage, the postmaster informed her, "You won't have to pay for this. The postal workers have taken up a special collection, and it will cover the cost of mailing all these and more of the next shipment!" He had deliberately sent her home without paying the day before so that the workers could determine the mailing cost and collect sufficient funds among themselves from all the shifts. It was their contribution to the effort to find Susie, a sign of their concern and compassion for our ordeal.*

*Through our own mailman, who knew Susie personally, postal delivery people across the nation were notified of her disappearance through their national newsletter and were asked to watch for her as they went about their delivery routes. Then, when the reward fund collection was announced, a special box number at the post office had to be set up to accommodate mailed donations. So the postal workers were well-aware of the situation, and especially of the poster project.

The Lost Child

I know I speak for all those involved when I say that that whole experience was an emotionally gratifying time for all of us. We were not free to divulge any of the recent developments, so all we could appeal to was the public's compassion. We were not disappointed! Everyone who contributed, in whatever way or amount, was responsible in a very special way for keeping Susie's face before the eyes and mind of her kidnapper, wherever he went; each and every person shared in bringing about the resolution of this case, because we know now that those posters made it impossible for the kidnapper to forget.

8

Standing Naked Before God

The Christmas holidays were upon us. Presuming that the posters had been distributed by now and hoping for that important call, we did not attend any festivities away from home. However, friends and relatives came to visit often, and amazingly, we had a lovely Christmas season. This was important to us, especially for the sake of Dan, Frank, Heidi, and Joe, who still remained children with individual needs and ongoing lives in the midst of our concern for the one who was lost.

Some new leads came in during this time as a result of the posters, but in each instance the child involved was determined not to be Susie, but rather another child in an unfortunate or bad circumstance. How I prayed for all those children whose life situations were far from ideal, and for all those parents from whom, or about whom, we had heard who also had children missing under dire circumstances. Some were unhappy about the services of the law enforcement agencies investigating their cases, some wished they could get more publicity. How grateful I was for God's providence for us thus far!

However, once Christmas was over and we had resumed our normal routine, the situation seemed to change. I began to be filled with a great resentment toward God. Thoughts and feelings had been forming in my mind that I'd tried to bury or dismiss, but I knew I could not ignore them any longer. Repression of strong emotions for a long time is most destructive to the human psyche, and I had reached a point where I feared my sanity was at stake. Besides, what good did it do to pretend, if God knew what was in my heart anyway? I recognized that I was going to have to acknowledge my feelings. I was going to have to "stand naked before God."

Other people had said it to me before, and I had brushed it off; now I had to ask it out loud of myself: "What kind of God would let something like this happen? What kind of loving Father would put us through all this?"

When Susie was first taken, my immediate reaction was that Satan had caused this evil, but that God would come to my rescue. However, as time went by and I pondered it more, I realized that God was mightier than Satan; Satan couldn't do anything unless God had allowed it. What kind of good God would have allowed anything as horrible as this to happen to people who had specifically asked for His blessing and protection? What kind of loving Father would have drawn us out to Montana, put us on top of the world, and then pulled it all out from under us? "I'm no saint, Lord, but what have I ever done to deserve this kind of punishment? And certainly an innocent and defenseless seven-year-old doesn't deserve to be taken away from the love and safety of her family!"

Even in natural terms, disregarding God's presumed protection, the kidnapper should not have been successful in taking Susie. There was an overhead light on in the campground. Dogs were tied up outside of tents and campers; yet none of them had barked. Just down the road past the park was a cement factory. All night long truck drivers on the way to get loads of cement stopped at the campground to have a cup of coffee at a picnic table or a drink of water at the well, and yet none of them had seen anything. A family with five children, all of them sleeping outside under the stars, were spread out on the lawn behind our tent. That was the side of the tent that was cut, the side where Susie was taken from, but none of them had seen or heard a thing. With all these circumstances against him, the kidnapper was still able to abduct my little girl! "What kind of God are You, anyway?"

Then I began to wonder if there really was a God at all. Maybe Susie's abduction was able to happen because there really wasn't a God to protect us, to prevent evil. Maybe the notion of God was just a psychological crutch some wise person dreamed up a long time ago to keep the human race in line. But the more I pursued this train of thought, the more despairing I became. Finally, I realized that without God I had no hope for my life, no hope for this world, no hope for Susie, and I could not bear that. The future became so hopelessly bleak that I knew I *wanted* to believe in God. And yet how could I believe in God when the night that Susie was taken seemed so totally devoid of His presence? Verse seven of Psalm 34 says, "The angel of the Lord encamps around those who fear him, and he delivers them." And Psalm 91:10–11 says, "No harm will befall you, no disaster will come near your tent. For he will command his angels concerning you to guard you in all your ways." That hadn't been true for us. What was I to believe?

I felt I was on the edge of a cliff, being pulled in both directions. When I looked over the edge, it was so black and bottomless that I was filled with terror and scrambled for safety. Then it seemed as though I was being pulled to a safe place. I recognized that if I was to stay safe, I was going to have to make a decision to believe in God, trust Him, and abide by that decision. If not, I would go over the edge into darkness.

At that point, I began to make an act of faith, with an

audible voice, in a God whose love did not seem to be discernible in my life any more. As I sat there in my room professing my faith that He was a loving Father, that He had allowed this only so that He could bring about a greater good, that He would give me all the grace and strength I needed to cope, that He would take care of Susie, that He would resolve her disappearance, there still a part of me that kept wishing for some special sign, some real confirmation that God was actually there. I felt He surely was asking a lot of me, considering the circumstances. I wanted to love Him, but that was so hard to do when, really, I only knew *of* Him. How could I truly love someone I didn't know personally? If only I could really know Him! But I felt this was a privilege reserved for the very holy, which I was not. And besides, if I already knew Him, then I would be making an act of fact, not an act of faith, and I knew I was being called to make an act of faith in a God who chose to be unseen, distant, and silent.

I continued to pray, and as my declaration grew more fervent in the increasing power of God's grace, and as it ceased to matter that He chose to seem absent—suddenly, He *was* there! In His mercy and kindness, God allowed me to experience His presence in a dramatic, mystical, supernatural way!

I felt as though I was swept up into His arms and, like a little child, lifted upon His lap. I was totally enveloped in what I can only call the Love of God. I could feel it physically around my flesh. The human mind cannot fathom the never-ending, limitless love of God, but I was instantly aware of how incredible was His love compared to my puny, conditional, feeble attempts to love. Yet even with my realization of that miserable failing, He made me feel precious beyond words as He held me against His bosom.

There was no way I, as a human with a finite mind,

could ever comprehend this God; His omnipotence and magnificence were beyond all my wildest dreams and imaginings. Without understanding how, I just knew He knew how many hairs were upon my head. There was absolutely no doubt that anyone who could love like that was an infinitely Superior Being who would certainly know those facts about me.

This marvelous God was also absolutely irresistible. I could not turn away from Him. My whole being was drawn to Him, and my heart was in a state of total surrender; my only desire was to be united with Him. Whatever He would ask of me, whatever the cost, I would say, "Yes!" instantly. Now I understood why God does not reveal Himself in His fullness to us on an everyday basis. To do so would be to renege on His gift of our free will, and He is that perfect gentleman who holds Himself distant so that we are always assured the freedom to choose Him or not.

My deepest and most meaningful impression of that encounter was my recognition of God as Father—not Almighty God, not Awesome Judge, but Father. I have a stepfather now whom I love as a real father, but I was raised by my natural father who died many years ago. If he, the father I had as a little girl, were to walk into a room where I was standing, I'd recognize him instantly—not as a man, but as my daddy, the man with whom I had lived, the man who took care of me, the man who loved me in a special way, the man to whom I entrusted my life. That was the experience I now had with my heavenly Father. It was as though I had been with Him before and *recognized* Him as my Father. But even the word "Father" is too formal. The relationship between us was so personal and intimate that I would have called Him "Daddy" had I spoken. And I remembered that when Jesus walked this earth, He called God "Abba" and "Abba" means "Daddy."

The Lost Child

And with that realization came the recognition that that's how He loved me—as His own dear child. He delighted to receive my love and trust. And thus, surely I could trust Him! Anyone who loved me like God did could be trusted with each and every moment of my life. Anyone who loved me like that would never do anything that would hurt me or be wrong for me. I was content just to rest in His presence.

I have no idea how long this extraordinary experience lasted, but finally it seemed to "fade." Suddenly I remembered something I wanted to ask Him.

Out in Montana there were some wonderful, Dutch Christians who came to the campground often and did so much for us, and who kept talking about Jesus as their personal Lord, their personal Savior, their personal Friend. I had been baptized as a Christian, raised in a Christian home, educated in Christian schools, and I certainly had been taught about Jesus. I knew He died for our sins and now sat at the right hand of God. But I did not relate to their talk about a personal relationship with Him; yet somehow I felt I *should*. Somehow I seemed to have missed something about Jesus. So now, as if to "catch God before He moved away," I called out to Him. "Help me learn what You want me to know about Jesus," I asked, and with that the experience ended.

As I sat there in my bedroom, I was overwhelmed with gratitude at this indescribable gift that had been given to one so unworthy as me. The words I've used are so woefully inadequate to explain such a supernatural, mystical experience. I surely could identify with Job when he said, "I know that you can do all things; no plan of yours can be thwarted. You asked, 'Who is this that obscures my counsel without knowledge?' Surely I spoke of things I did not understand, things too wonderful for me to know. . . . My ears had heard of you but now my eyes have seen you. Therefore I despise myself and repent in dust and ashes'' (42:2—6).

I still had no answers about Susie, and I still had to walk in faith and obedience in that regard; but now I had come to that point to which Job had to come. I was finally truly willing to acknowledge that God was God and I was only a human being; He knew what He was doing, and I was the least able to judge. More importantly, I wanted Him to be my God; I wanted Him to be my Father; I wanted Him to be Lord of this situation; and I was willing to abide with whatever He allowed, because, by His grace, I knew I could trust His love for Susie, for me, for all of us.

This extraordinary blessing was granted to me in January; Susie had been taken the previous June. We'd already been waiting for six months; but we still had a long way to go!

9

No More Than I Can Handle

Days, weeks, and months dragged by. Leads and suspects continued to surface, to no avail. Then in late winter, an eighteen-year-old girl from a small town close to the campground in Montana disappeared from her home. A few weeks later, her car was found hidden in an old barn on an old abandoned ranch a few miles from the campground. Her charred remains were also found on that same property. Because of some similarities and the proximity to our situation, everything that turned up in the investigation of her case was checked out in regard to Susie's case.

The F.B.I. accumulated a voluminous file by any standards. They maintained close contact with us, keeping us posted on any significant developments. Much of what they did will probably never be known to us, as they tried to protect us from the emotional turmoil of raising our hopes with innumerable new leads only to have them dashed to the ground. However, we were always kept informed of the progress in resolving all the leads that came to us personally via phone or mail, and again and again we were disappointed as the information was determined to be irrelevant to our situation. Unfortunately, that was something I just couldn't get accustomed to, and each time was a trial of faith.

Over and over again I had to remind myself that my Father wouldn't give me more than I could handle with the help of His grace. Each morning I had to remind myself that I would be able to endure that day or God would not have allowed it. I had to believe His promises to me that I would not be tested beyond my strength; I had to stand on them and refuse to listen to Satan's lies or give in to my human inclination to despair.

Certain situations were more difficult than others. Any western scene, whether on television or in a magazine, made my heart ache unbearably. So also did the sight of any kind of camping gear, and it seemed that every store I went into was selling something along that line. The sight of Susie's friends would pitch me right into desolation, and for months I was absolutely unable to listen to any kind of music, always such an important part of my life, without tears streaming down my cheeks and an almost complete loss of emotional control.

But the most difficult time was at night. Sleep was often long in coming as I lay there, listening, waiting, hoping that Susie might be returned, as she'd been taken, under cover of darkness. When she wasn't, it was hard to control the imaginings of my mind as to what her nights might be like. Even after sleep finally came, my dreams were filled with the search for my little girl. Sometimes she was found and there was joyous reunion with us; sometimes her rescue came too late. There were many nightmares which left me drained and tired the next day—especially one, in which she suffered and died, the stark horror of which woke me and made sleep impossible. That gruesome dream occurred only once, but it went on and on like a ghastly movie which I was forced to watch and could not stop, and it couldn't have been more abominable!

Some days my hope really wore thin, usually after being disappointed by another false lead. On those occasions the only thing that "worked" for me was to pray the Twenty-second Psalm, the one Jesus prayed on the cross. It was effective because it met me where I was: "My God, my God, why have you forsaken me? . . . and took me to where I should be: For dominion is the Lord's. . . . And to him my soul shall live. . . . Let the coming generation be told of the Lord that they may proclaim to a people yet to be born the justice he has shown" (vv. 1, 29–32 NAB). I spent a great deal of time in prayer and reading Scripture.

For the most part our children were kept abreast of each new development because we felt it healthier to keep an open environment in which we could all share our feelings and support one another. Besides, certain phone calls and the comings and goings of the F.B.I. agents were so obvious that to keep the children uninformed would have been not only difficult, but also detrimental to them. Certainly it was a time of anguished waiting for all the family, but I'm grateful Bill and the children had the benefit of the distractions of job and school. Although it was not always easy to give themselves to those activities, and many times Bill had to be called home from work because of some new development, for the most part it did help to occupy their minds with other thoughts and let them live a somewhat normal lifestyle.

God also had sent a few very special people into our life, folks from Montana and Michigan who had themselves endured horrible tragedies. They were an inspiration for me, and I kept telling myself that if they could survive their trials, then it must be possible for me to survive also. They were proof to me of God's faithfulness, and I clung to that hope.

As a young girl, I had always had a special appreciation and love for Mary, the mother of our Lord. I considered her to be the quintessence of Christian womanhood, and as I grew up I tried to model myself after her. However, now my feelings toward her began to change.

Her young Son had been lost, too, but only for three days, and then He was found, safe and sound in the temple. My little girl had been gone for months, and God alone knew how she was or when, or even if, I'd ever get her back. I found myself filled with bitterness toward Mary. She was able to take her Son home and care for Him again. She didn't know what it was like to give her child up to only-God-knows-what. Oh, how I resented her privilegedness! Yet, in the midst of my bitterness I knew my attitude was not right, and my heart was heavy.

Shortly thereafter, my washing machine broke down —my brand-new washing machine—and the repairman could not come for a number of days. Feeling aggravated and inconvenienced, I bundled up my family's dirty clothes and drove to the nearest laundromat. After starting the washers, I looked around for a magazine with which to occupy myself. Picking up an old and tattered copy of *Reader's Digest,* I scanned through it, searching for an interesting title. One article stood out: it was written by a layman and was about Mary and what could be learned about her from the Scriptures.

Most of it was "old stuff" to me, but then the writer pointed out something I'd never realized before. Chapter three of Mark's Gospel tells how Jesus' relatives became convinced He was out of His mind and went to bring Him home so they could take care of Him. When they arrived at the place He was staying, there was a large crowd gathered. Jesus was informed that His mother and brothers were outside asking for Him, but instead of going out to see them, He turned to the people encircling Him. "Here are my mother and my brothers! Whoever does God's will is my brother and sister and mother," He said. Just imagine, the article went on, how Mary must have felt. Here was her beloved Son, by all appearances behaving very strangely and making all kinds of radical-sounding pronouncements, and she could not get to Him. Worse yet, He did not seem willing to even speak with her, let alone return home with her.

Imagine how painful it was for her to have to leave without Him. Was He really sick? What was happening? If only she could have talked to Him, held Him for just a minute. It was all so difficult to understand. Now she knew she could no longer make any kind of familial claim on Jesus. She couldn't take Him home and care for Him. She had to give her Son up to only-God-knows-what. She had to let Him go to serve His Father's purpose for His life.

As I sat there trying to finish the article through the tears streaming from my eyes, I knew it was not just coincidence that I had found that magazine. God had an important lesson for me to learn: Just as He understood completely the sacrifice Mary was required to make, so He understood my suffering, too. And I realized it was important to Jesus that I appreciate the anguish of His mother, for she, too, had walked the road of painful separation from her child.

As the Lord spoke to my heart through that magazine article, I also began to see that Susie, too, had been chosen to serve a special purpose for her Father. I began to understand that I was being called to relinquish all claims on my youngest daughter. It was difficult, but gradually my prayers began to change. To prepare myself for what God might ask of me, I offered her to the Father every day. I was determined that no one would take her from me, but that I would willingly give her back to God, to whom she really belonged anyhow. Now I also identified with Abraham, who was asked to sacrifice his child to God; yet with that came the hope that God would restore, as He did Isaac, my child to my arms. How I longed for that to come true!

10

Is This Susie's Mom?

It was nearly the end of June, 1974—nearly one year since Susie had been taken. The Associated Press office in Montana wanted to run a story in the western papers about us, about what it was like to live for a whole year without knowing the whereabouts of our little girl. They sent a reporter and photographer from their Detroit office to interview me for the article.

After we had completed the formal interview and were having coffee in my kitchen, the reporter said to me, "Mrs. Jaeger, I just don't understand your kind of faith. If that same thing had happened to my daughter, neither I nor any of my family would ever set foot in a church again."

"Believe me, I understand why you would feel like that," I responded. But I also felt led to share with him all the ways the Lord had cared for us during this time, all the grace He had showered upon me, and my belief that God had not caused this, but allowed it only because He was going to bring a greater good from it. I also told him how God had enabled me to desire a forgiving heart. As our conversation ended, I added, "I would give anything to speak to the kidnapper myself. My heart aches for him and how he must feel." Unable to understand or share my feelings, the reporter could only shake his head, though he was most kind and respectful during our talk.

Information put out on Teletype, as this story was, can

sometimes be subject to distortion, exaggeration, deletion, misrepresentation, or anything else which suits each local editor's intention. In most instances, we had been blessed with reasonably accurate publicity; but this time we were especially blessed. The Psalms tell us that God inhabits the praise of His people; truly He honored my words in this interview and was present when this article was written and printed.

The AP reporter had composed the piece conscientiously true to my statements, and in a small town close to the campground in Montana, it was printed with my hopes and feelings quoted verbatim. Scheduled for publication on the anniversary of Susie's disappearance, somehow it was published the day before, and the kidnapper read these words in his paper: "I guess I feel sorry for him. Anyone who could do a thing like that can't be happy. I would like to talk to him, to find out why. I guess I'll never get the chance." Unable to resist the challenge, in the very early hours of the next morning, one year exactly to the minute since her abduction, the man who had taken my Susie called our home!

Even though we were sound asleep, I heard the phone immediately. Middle-of-the-night phone calls were not too unusual for us now. Sometimes people would furtively wait till long after dark to call and name a possible suspect. Racing to the phone in the dark, I tripped over a stool and hurt my foot quite badly. Yet as I picked up the receiver, the pain suddenly subsided.

I was completely awake and alert as I heard the man's voice ask, "Is this Susie's mom? I'm the guy that took her from you exactly a year ago, to the minute, today," he said. I was terrified that I wouldn't be able to hear another sound for the noise of my heart pounding in my ears.

Groping for words, I asked where Susie was, if she was alive.

"Yes, she is ma'am," he replied, and went on to say, "I've gotten used to having her with me and we've had quite a time together, traveling all over the West."

Suddenly the phone went dead. I was stunned and overcome with disappointment—to have waited so long only to have it end so quickly! Moments later, while I was still standing next to the phone trying to reconcile myself with the futility of that brief conversation, the phone rang again. Thinking it to be the F.B.I. who had been notified of the kidnapper's call by my oldest son from a neighbor's phone, I was startled to hear the same man's voice apologizing that we'd been cut off.

After carefully describing every phone call about which only we and the F.B.I. and the real kidnapper could know, he said, baiting me, "I know you're waiting to hear this," and went on to identify Susie by her "humpy fingernails." He claimed to have almost wiped out of her mind all memory of her previous life through the use of psychotherapy. "She's like my own little girl now, and she loves me like her own father."

As our conversation went on, I became increasingly aware of a strong feeling of concern for this smug and taunting man. Without realizing it, he began to respond to this unexpected attitude in me. The more questions I asked, the less defensive he became.

When I asked, "Where is Susie right now?" he said she was up in his cabin sleeping. "But don't worry about her being left alone, because I'm not far from there," he reassured me. Oh, how I prayed this was true. I inquired about her health. "I had to hurt her when I pulled her from the tent, but that was the only time. I've taken good care of her." He went on to say that to disguise her identity he had dyed her hair and changed the style.

I kept trying to coax more information from him which would have proven she was still alive, but he refused, saying he needed it to authenticate any further calls he might have to make. I was so torn—part of me wanted to believe that all he said was true, and part of me knew it couldn't possibly be.

Yet, in spite of my anguish and frustration, as I desperately searched for ways to reach him, there rose within me an overwhelming sense of compassion. I knew that it had not originated in me, but that this feeling now had become my own. It was as if a part of me was standing aside, watching objectively, and was able to see a miracle taking place within my heart. God had truly given me the capacity to forgive this man! Though I was not blinded to the possible realities of Susie's condition, I was also fraught with concern for this deeply troubled man.

As I questioned him about his care of Susie, his voice quavered a few times, though he maintained she had come to love him as her own father. When I asked, "What can we do to help you? Do you know I've been praying for you?" he seemed unable to speak. At one point, in a barely audible voice, he said, "I'd like to have this burden off my soul." I wasn't sure what his burden was, but oh, how I wanted to help him.

My mind was divided: *Susie is still alive and I must convince him to return her to us—All my words and pleas are just a waste of time because Susie is already dead.* Regardless of my inner turmoil, I felt I must convince this man that I believed all he said.

I remembered to ask about something that had puzzled everyone. "How did you happen to take Susie? How did you know there was a little girl in our tent? Had you seen her earlier?" I queried.

"I came by the tent during the night, and I heard her and her sister talking," he answered, "but I waited until they fell asleep again before I took her." Yes, Heidi had mentioned that conversation when Susie was first taken.

Once when I said we would do anything he asked to get Susie back, he said he was working on a plan to get the $14,000 in reward money being offered. That's when I knew the reward posters had served a purpose. They'd constantly confronted him with the unresolved situation; they wouldn't let him forget.

An environment of forgiveness and compassion had been created by God's grace, and it was softening his hostile heart; but I sensed that the conversation was coming to an end. Yet I was no closer to having Susie back than I was before his call. Suddenly, there was a disturbance on the line.

"What was that?" he asked with alarm. "Did you hear that? Is someone else listening?" Then accusingly, "Did you have the line tapped? Is this call being traced?" Not wanting to lie, I talked on as though unaware of any sound, and amazingly, he calmed down immediately. However, when the noise started up again a few minutes later, he became quite nervous. "It's time to hang up, but I want you to say good-by first."

I had absolutely no intention of terminating this conversation. So pretending not to hear, I asked him again to please release Susie, giving examples of how he could accomplish this. "Or at least give me proof that she's still alive by letting me talk to her over the phone. Or take her picture and send it to me." Challenged by my requests, his edginess seemed to disappear, and I resumed my efforts to win him over. He was my one link to Susie and I had waited a whole year for this opportunity; I was not about to let him go if I could help it!

I asked questions about his life with Susie during the past year: "Where did you take Susie when you were traveling? How did you keep her hidden?"

"I took her to Disneyland and to the San Diego Zoo," he replied. "I only had to keep her hidden when I was at home. The rest of the time she was just a little girl with her father."

The Lost Child

Again and again he said it was time to say good-by, only to be dissuaded by more questions, more appeals to his heart, more pleas. If he really did love her as a father, he must be concerned about her welfare. "You can't move about as you'd like," I pointed out. "How can she get an education? There's no way you can give her a normal life."

Finally, no longer able to restrain the emotion in my voice and heart, I begged him to give Susie back, pleaded with him not to make me wait any longer as I'd had to wait all this long year. "She's my little girl and no one can love her or care for her as I can. I brought her into this world. I am her mother and I have a right to her!"

As I stopped to gain control of myself, I realized, to my surprise, that the kidnapper was sobbing—sobbing in seemingly unbearable anguish. Somewhere in the depths of his being he was suffering torment that I could never begin to understand. I was allowed to hear that, and I was grateful for this insight into his heart, grateful to know that some part of his spirit abhorred the act he had committed. Finally, in a broken, tearful voice, he said, "Good-by," and the connection was severed.

11

David

Helpless and drained, I stood holding the silent telephone receiver. My only link to Susie had been broken, and again I was left with nothing. As my mind struggled to accept this, I began to focus on what was still happening.

When the phone had rung, Bill had been awakened too. He had been with me during the entire call, which we now ascertained to have lasted over an hour! Incredibly, for all his fear that the call was being traced and that he would be discovered, the kidnapper had continued to talk to me that long.

Another indication, for me, that the Lord was present was the fact that even though I'd been wakened from a sound sleep, I had had the presence of mind to start the tape recorder before answering the phone. So not only did we get the complete conversation on tape, but because of the way the recorder was set up, Bill had been able to hear both sides of the conversation as it took place.

Dan and Heidi had been awakened by the ringing of the phone, and Bill had sent them across the street to use a neighbor's phone to inform the F.B.I. The agents had immediately notified telephone company personnel responsible for tracing calls. By the time I got off the phone, they had already determined that the call had come from someplace in Sarasota, Florida.

I began to get excited, remembering how successfully other calls, crank calls, had been traced in just a few minutes' time. Any moment now they would be calling to let us know the exact point of origin of the kidnapper's call. Any moment now I would know if Susie really was just a short distance away from him, sleeping in his cabin. Any moment now I could be talking to her on the phone!

We were surprised that the call hadn't come from out West, but if Susie really was in Florida, it would work out better when we got her back. My youngest sister, a familiar face to Susie, lived there and could stay with her until we could fly down ourselves.

Two F.B.I. agents came over as the sun came up, and as we all sat drinking coffee and waiting for word to come of the exact location, they listened to the taped recording of the call. They, too, were convinced of its authenticity. Finally we heard that there would be a delay in tracing the call further, as there were no telephone company personnel on duty during the night in Sarasota. Everything was operated electronically. In order to get at the equipment to continue the trace, a supervisor had to be brought in to open the building. Unfortunately, timing was critical; the more time that elapsed, the less chance there was of a successful trace. It was so exasperating to have to deal with this delay at such a crucial time.

Because this day was the anniversary of Susie's disappearance, I had planned to attend a daily Eucharistic liturgy in my church on this morning. Now I hated to leave our house. But the day before I had agreed to be interviewed by a local television station, and they were to meet me at the church. If I did not show up, the TV crew might come to the house, and at this critical time, the less people who knew what was going on, the better.

So, leaving my husband and the agents to wait for word of further developments in Sarasota, Florida, I went to church at the appointed time. During the service, a strong sense of peace and trust in God enveloped my heart. I knew that other relatives and friends were praying also on this day, June 25—praying for all of us and for God's purpose to be served.

Once the interview was over, I hurried home. The situation had not changed; they were still trying to continue the trace, although it was beginning to look as though it would not be successful. However, the F.B.I. in Florida were out in full force, doing whatever they could to determine who and where the kidnapper was if he was in Florida, and if Susie was with him.

The agents left our home for their office to make copies of the recording to send to the F.B.I. in Montana, who had already been notified that the anniversary call had occurred. Once again, as it became obvious that the trace could not be completed, I had to resign myself to more disappointment, more waiting.

Now I understood why God's peace had been poured out so fully in my heart as I knelt before the altar at church. I was going to need it to endure still more. Truly God can work most powerfully when we are the weakest. Part of me was screaming, "Enough is enough! This cross is totally intolerable, completely unbearable! Have mercy, have mercy!" And yet another part, made strong by the grace of God, knew simply that it was not yet God's timing and that He would take care of me and keep me going until it was. That was the attitude I was enabled to maintain; and what God did for me, He did for the rest of my family.

We were also reassured that the fifty-thousand-dollar ransom money, deposited in a special account a year ago, was still available to us at any time should the kidnapper call again and want to complete exchange arrangements. If only he would!

One of the ideas that occurred to everyone involved was that Sarasota was winter headquarters for circus people. Circuses have side shows, side shows often travel with rodeos, and Montana has a lot of rodeos. The kidnapper had said he had moved around a lot with Susie. Perhaps he had been involved in that kind of work and now had taken her back to his home in Florida.

Following through on this possibility, the F.B.I. began to question circus people. A few thought they had seen a man with a little girl in questionable circumstances. The problem was that people who work with circuses and rodeos rarely are in one place for long. Soon there were leads going out to cities and towns all over the United States.

Meanwhile, the F.B.I. agents in Montana were listening to the tape of the anniversary call, taking it apart word by word, checking for any discernible sounds in the background which might help them identify the location of the phone. Providentially, the attitude God had given me toward the kidnapper had encouraged him to let down some of his defenses and speak more openly than he had intended. So with their expertise the agents were able to discern certain vital clues: places the caller said he'd been, his mobile lifestyle, and the sound of his voice.

The clues seemed to point to a young man named David who lived in a town close to the campground where Susie had been taken and who had been one of the suspects in the initial stages of the investigation. Now the F.B.I. began to gather all the information they could uncover about him, while he, unaware, went about his normal routine. Of course, the first thing they needed to determine was whether there was any child in his care, either in his home or in some hidden place. Again, all we could do was wait.

One afternoon about a month or so after the first anniversary of Susie's disappearance, I received a call from the telephone company in Montana. They said a woman was in their office checking about her telephone bill which contained charges for two long-distance calls, one very brief and one lengthy, made to our residence in Michigan in the middle of the night on the anniversary of Susie's abduction. This woman claimed she had never made these calls, and the telephone company was trying to verify her statement. Elatedly recognizing that this could be the "key" for which we'd been praying, I declared that I had not received any calls from this woman, but I asked that the F.B.I. in Montana be notified about the circumstance immediately. Because of the widespread publicity about Susie, the telephone company representative had recognized my name and was most willing to comply with my request.

No one was ever able to determine how the anniversary call was traced to Florida. But soon the F.B.I. made contact to inform us of their investigation of this latest development. They had spoken to the woman and were convinced that neither she nor anyone in her family had made the anniversary call. What they did discover was that this family, who lived in town, had a cabin out in the hills in which they lived while working their ground or harvesting their crops. Outside the cabin were bare uninsulated telephone wires onto which a handset could have been clipped and from which a call could have been made. (One of the background sounds on the taped recording had been identified as crickets chirping.) Underneath the wires were truck tire tracks, still clear enough to determine the brand of tire. The tracks indicated that the tires were fairly new, and so the tire dealer in a nearby town was questioned. The young man, David, who seemed to be implicated by the anniversary call, had recently purchased this type of tire for his truck. He had, when in the Marines, been trained in communications and would know how to operate a handset. And he had worked as a handyman on this piece of property set back in the hills and thus knew of its whereabouts.

The Lost Child

It was also now determined that David had been in the little town in Wyoming on the same day that my oldest son had received the call from the kidnapper which had been traced to that place. His voice and manner of speaking seemed to be identical to that of the caller. And finally, because he had been a rejected suitor, David had been a suspect in the still-unresolved murder of the eighteen-year-old girl who disappeared eight months after Susie. However, there was no evidence as yet to uphold the charge, and David had passed a polygraph exam on that occasion.

Even though this was all circumstantial evidence, the F.B.I. went to David and advised him to obtain the services of an attorney; they told him that he was considered to be the prime suspect in the kidnapping of Susan Jaeger.

At last, it seemed the end was in sight. We had been waiting for more than a year; now finally there was a real possibility that the kidnapper had been discovered!

However, along with this came terrible reality: we began to realize that Susie would not be returned to us. Though there was not as yet proof of her death and many questions remained unanswered, Bill and I began to prepare ourselves and the children for what seemed to be inevitable.

12

Seeking God's Justice

On the counsel of his attorney, David agreed to take a polygraph exam in order to prove his innocence. When Susie was first taken, he had been one of many possible suspects because he lived alone and was unable to prove his whereabouts the night she disappeared. He had passed the lie detector test then, and so he did now.

Not satisfied with the results, the F.B.I. approached him about taking a "truth serum" injection. Again, in the belief that it would exonerate him, and encouraged by his attorney, David agreed. In a controlled situation set up in a hospital in the presence of the F.B.I., David's attorney, and a doctor, the drug was administered. Again, no incrimination.

Bolstered by this, and feeling self-confident and secure in his ability to outsmart everyone, David continued to insist on his innocence. But as the tape recordings of his calls, his background including known violent episodes, and his personality were being analyzed by psychiatrists and psychoanalysts, it became more and more apparent that David was a very sick young man; that he was indeed psychotic and dangerous.

With the cooperation of his attorney, the F.B.I. now attempted to re-create the circumstances of the anniversary call. A partial script of the conversation, taken from the tape recording, was to be read by David and four other men, some of whom were his relatives with similar-sounding voices, during a phone call placed from the cabin in the hills of Montana to our home in Michigan, with F.B.I. agents present in both places.

The callers were identified only as #1, #2, #3, #4, and #5. I was to listen to them through the telephone receiver as I had the night of the anniversary call, and Bill was to listen through the recorder. The purpose of this activity was to determine if we could each positively identify one of these voices as the voice heard on the anniversary, the voice of the man who had identified Susie by her "humpy fingernails."

The F.B.I., always concerned about our welfare, were sorry to require our participation, but it was necessary and we understood this. To relieve some of the tension, we joked with the agents about dressing in our night clothes so as to really make it authentic, but in my heart I prayed that I would be able to maintain my composure as I heard words of that conversation repeated over and over. However, I felt certain that I would never forget the voice.

And truly, as soon as I heard David, though he was identified to me only as #2, I knew I was listening to the kidnapper. My husband and I had been told not to signify recognition of any voice to each other; it was important that we individually come to our conclusion. When the call was terminated, we each had to privately give a statement to the agents present in our home. Only after this was done were we free to compare reactions. Both of us had unhesitatingly identified #2 as the caller.

It had been hoped that David, in repeating the words of that crucial conversation, might be moved or disturbed sufficiently to break down or somehow incriminate himself. That did not happen—not even later when he was informed that we had identified his voice as the kidnapper's. However, it became obvious that his inner security was beginning to be undermined; occasionally as he went about his business in town he appeared very agitated for no apparent reason. I hated the fact that he had to go through this because I knew how disturbed he was. I prayed fervently that his heart would change soon for his sake as well as ours.

On the night of the day David had taken the truth serum test, an attempt was made to abduct a child from a different campground in another part of Montana. Though the man was frightened away before he could take the child, it was a horrifying confirmation of the conclusions being reached by the experts. David was known to have been in the area (the hospital where the test was conducted was there) and the description given by witnesses to the attempted abduction matched his description. Later, newspaper clippings announcing the presence of many children in that particular campground at that particular time, and a map with special markings (location of camp dwellings, a hiding place for his truck, good "cover" areas, etc.) were found in his possession, further linking him to the foiled kidnap attempt. As a result, law enforcement people began to keep him under such surveillance as was legally permissible.

It became very clear that David, in his terrible sickness, was a threat to the community. Consequently, it was imperative to insure a successful prosecution of the charge of Susie's abduction. Unless this happened, David would be acquitted and released into society again, free to harm another child.

The F.B.I. had accumulated a wealth of circumstantial evidence: David's new truck tires matched the tire marks left at the scene of the call; he had been present at the restaurant in the small town in Wyoming at the same time as the call received from there by my son; his background, which included some violent episodes; and our identification of his voice. And even though David had passed the polygraph and truth serum tests, there was one piece of positively incriminating evidence: the laboratory-verified match of

The Lost Child

David's voiceprint on tape as recorded over a telephone with the voiceprint of the anniversary caller, who had identified Susie by her fingernails. At that time this was a relatively new type of evidence permitted in the courtroom, and as such needed the testimony of a nationally reknown expert in this field, someone not affiliated with the F.B.I. There was one man considered sufficiently qualified to be called as a witness and who was willing to do so, but he was already tied up in litigation. We would have to wait till he was available.

By now, I had come to understand that God's idea of justice is not punishment, but restoration. For the community's sake, David's identification and apprehension were necessary. But for David's sake, I saw his arrest and incarceration not as an opportunity to seek revenge or even a "just" punishment, but as the only means to provide him with the psychiatric help he would never even acknowledge he needed, let alone seek. To this end I prayed that God's justice would be done for David, that he would be restored by whatever means of healing God chose to use.

Paradoxically, everyone's concern was that once arrested, David might attempt suicide. This would be characteristic behavior for someone with his particular type of mental illness. Not only did I abhor this possibility for him, but if he were to do so before acknowledging his responsibility for Susie's disappearance, we would never know what had become of her. So when the F.B.I. asked me to come out to Montana, at their expense, to talk with David face-to-face, I eagerly assented. Their intent for my mission was to obtain as much information as possible from David before he was arrested. He had been disturbed and deeply moved once before while talking to me on the phone; perhaps I could get through to him again.

While my parents stayed with our children, Bill and I flew to Montana. It is difficult to explain my feelings as we landed. I was exhilarated to be back in this beautiful place with so many wonderful people, and at the same time I was filled with the deepest grief at the loss of my little girl. In this place I had experienced the happiest moments of my life— and the saddest. I was grateful that my husband, always strong and courageous, was with me.

We were met at the airport by the agent in charge of the investigation and in whose home we would be staying. The gracious hospitality of this fine man and his lovely wife did much to put us at ease and enable me to relax in this tense situation.

The next morning, in his attorney's office, I came face to face with the man I was certain had kidnapped my Susie. David was in his mid-twenties, not very tall but powerfully built, clean-cut and polite. As I looked into his deep, dark eyes for the first time, I had no doubt that he was a sick, horribly sick man. I should have been frightened, but I wasn't. The F.B.I. had done their best to prepare me, and I had prayed fervently before our meeting—all the previous night, in fact. So I felt strong and in the presence of the Lord who loved us both. But David also had had preparation. He had been told I was coming, since he had to agree to the meeting, and had had time to prepare himself to be strong and confident in his stance of innocence.

It had been suggested that a strong, direct approach might be more likely to intimidate David, and that's how I tried to handle it, but he was ready for me and in control of his defenses. His attorney sat unobtrusively in the corner, recording the conversation on tape, but David seemed to take support from his presence and kept up his mental guard. He refused to acknowledge the anniversary call, repeatedly stating he knew nothing about Susie's disappearance. I was persistent in my insistence that he was the kidnapper, but at the end of an hour and a half, he was still declaring he was innocent, and the conversation was terminated.

As David stood to leave, he reached out to shake hands with me. I grasped his hand with both of mine and tried one last time. "David, I know you're the man who took Susie, and the authorities will be able to prove it in court, but it would be so much better for you if you admit it now. There's no escaping the truth!"

"I'm really sorry, Mrs. Jaeger," he replied. "I wish I could help you, but I don't know anything about your little girl." With that, David walked away. It took all the control I had by God's grace to release his hand and allow him out of my sight.

In the afternoon we visited some of the dear friends in the area who had kept in touch all the past year. They had no idea why we were in town and simply presumed we had come out to check on the investigation. Few people, either in Michigan or Montana, were aware that there was now a prime suspect in the case. It was a sensitive situation: the F.B.I. agents were trying to pressure David into acknowledging what he'd done to Susie; and yet too much pressure could, because of his psychosis, cause him to attempt suicide. For a whole year we had sought publicity to keep Susie's disappearance before the public; now we were seeking to avoid it at all costs!

Late that night we decided to call David on the phone, at the F.B.I.'s suggestion. He would be home alone; perhaps he might respond more favorably in this circumstance. But again, claiming someone probably was listening in on the conversation, he was very careful what he said. He insisted he was ignorant of any information about Susie. No matter what ploy I used, his guard was up; he would not admit anything. However, in spite of the fact that he seemed to become impatient and somewhat irritated by my accusations, before we hung up I persuaded him to meet me the next afternoon, just the two of us alone, in the small building out of which he ran his own business as a general contractor.

I could sense the concern of the F.B.I. for my safety and I was aware that this could be a dangerous undertaking. David knew I was a threat to him, and in his aggravated state just might try to hurt me, prone to violence as he was.

As I prepared to meet him though, the Lord took all the fear from my heart. For one thing, I knew the law enforcement people would have me covered as closely as possible and that Bill would be nearby. He was swift and agile and would come rapidly to my rescue if necessary. Moreover, although I had been called to Montana by the F.B.I., I knew also that I had been called to Montana by God. I was being given the opportunity to say face-to-face to David, a real person and not just a voice on the phone, "I forgive you, and more than that, God forgives you, David, whatever you've done, if only you will accept it!" I knew our Father wanted this young man to know that he was as precious to Him as Susie was.

"Please acknowledge Susie's death," I begged as I stood there alone before him, "so that it can be a gift of life for you, so that you can receive the help you need to become the man you were created to be, not unhappy and lonely as you are now." Saint Paul says, "We are God's work of art, created in Christ Jesus to live the good life as from the beginning he had meant us to live it" (Eph. 2:10 JB). This could be true for David, too, and I prayed that he would believe it. But his response to me was, as could be expected, "I don't need any help. Nothing's wrong with me. I'm not sick!"

I talked to David for a long time. He had been observed earlier in the day and had appeared to be quite agitated, but now he was calm. "I wish I could help you," he said once again, but he protested he knew nothing. I knew he was afraid I was "bugged" with a secret microphone, which I was not, so he was cautious about what he said, and very controlled. Occasionally I saw a visible reaction to some of the statements I made about the attempted abduction of the child on the night of the truth serum test and the death of the eighteen-year-old girl, but I was unable to verbally catch him off-guard.

Finally, I realized that this conversation also would be fruitless in terms of information about my daughter. I could only pray that my words and the Lord's forgiveness would be received by David. My spirit ached for this wounded and broken soul whose loneliness and torment God had now allowed me to understand to some degree. Behind all his defensiveness was a man filled with fear, humiliation, pain, and guilt. Only God knew how much in control of his actions he was; only God could judge his heart.

But as I walked away, I knew that a miracle had happened within me. I knew David was responsible for taking Susie from us and for taking her life. Even in the face of overwhelming evidence, I had not been able to convince him to reveal Susie's fate or whereabouts, and he was causing me to feel I had failed my family, the F.B.I., and even God. Yet, I could not deny that God's love had been placed in my heart for that young man. If only I could have reached him with it. Had I? Would I ever know?

13

The Final Report

The F.B.I. agents had been very concerned about me all this time. They made certain I knew that a successful prosecution of the case was not dependent upon the outcome of my meetings with David. Still, my heart was heavy and I struggled against hopelessness as we left Montana and returned to Michigan.

Once home, all I could do was pray that somehow David would respond to the forgiveness and healing which God was holding out to him. As for the F.B.I., they proceeded to prepare for his arrest, waiting for the voiceprint expert to be free and available to testify on our behalf.

The week after Bill and I returned from Montana marked one year since the first time David had called us, the time when he spoke to our oldest son. Knowing now how meticulously David kept records, and because it had been so important to him to call us on the anniversary of Susie's disappearance, one year to the minute, we knew there was a good chance that he would call again on this anniversary. We discussed the possibility beforehand with the F.B.I. and everything was put in readiness just in case. If he called at the same time as before, it would be early evening.

On the morning of that day, a weekday, I was the only one in the house when the phone rang. Bill was at work, the children at school, and my folks, still visiting from Arizona, were camped in their trailer on our property. My dad had gone to the store; my mother was out in the trailer.

"Will you accept a long-distance call from a Mr. Travis?" asked the operator. "Yes," I replied. We were still receiving collect long-distance calls from all sorts of people, and we still accepted them, just in case they had some important information. But as "Mr. Travis" came on the line, I recognized David's voice immediately!

We had prearranged a signal with my folks in case they were ever needed in a hurry; as I put the fluorescent orange card in the window I prayed my mother, whom I knew was sitting down at her sewing machine, would look up and out her window and see it. In an instant she was through her door and running toward the house! As she entered the kitchen, she understood exactly what was happening and dashed to another phone to notify the F.B.I.

Meanwhile, I carried on a conversation with David. It soon became apparent that his intent was to convince me that this man to whom I was now speaking was the real kidnapper, not the man who was under suspicion in Montana.

(We would later learn that David had come home the night before, turned off the lights as if retiring, then slipped out a back window, crept across a field, and left town in another man's vehicle which was parked in David's warehouse. After driving rapidly all night, he had reached Salt Lake City, Utah, and called us, through the operator, knowing that the call would be traced, so that the F.B.I. would think that the "real" kidnapper was in Utah, not Montana where David was. He was desperately trying to divert suspicion from himself.)

But I had not the slightest doubt that I was speaking to David. When I called him by name, he said, "David? Who's David? Why do you keep calling me David?" Then angrily he asked, "Why did you tape the anniversary call?"

After this major slip in his disguise, I backed off a bit in order to keep him on the phone and began asking superficial questions. "Can you identify Susie? Have you come up with arrangements for an exchange for ransom?"

After mentioning her "humpy fingernails," he announced, "This time I can prove that I really have Susie, but you can only listen to her, not ask her any questions." I heard what sounded like a phone booth door opening and then a child's voice saying, "He's a nice man, mommy. I'm sitting on his lap." But it was not Susie's voice.

I began calling him David again, and as he realized that his scheme had failed, he became tense and frantic. He totally incriminated himself by blurting out many things that David had discussed with me or the F.B.I., things which only David would have known. Finally, realizing what he'd done in his panic, he said, "You're never gonna get your daughter back!" and slammed the receiver down!

I was terrified. I knew he did not have my daughter, but he had some child there with him, and in his sick mind she could now become Susie. Another child could be hurt—or worse.

In the meantime, the F.B.I. in Montana had determined that David was nowhere to be found. While he and I were still talking on the phone, the call had been traced to a motel in Salt Lake City. Within minutes, agents were on the scene, but David had already left the premises. An all-points bulletin was put out immediately between Montana and Utah for any missing child and David. I waited and prayed.

This call, too, had been taped, and F.B.I. agents were soon at our home to pick it up and make copies to send to Montana and their laboratory. They were able to determine that the child's voice I had heard was not of a child present with David as he made the call, but was a tape recording he played for me over the phone. (This was confirmed later when the tape was found.)

The Lost Child

Late in the day, David appeared back in his hometown. When he was approached by the law enforcement officers, he insisted he'd been "around" all day, that they must have just missed him as he went from job to job. But this last phone call was totally incriminating; it was the kind of concrete evidence the F.B.I. needed for a successful prosecution. They no longer needed to wait for the voiceprint expert. Moreover, it was a strong indication of just how sick and dangerous David really was!

After a flurry of legal activity, the agent in charge of the investigation in Montana called our home to advise that David would be arrested in the morning. He had not yet confessed nor divulged any information about Susie, but it was now imperative that he be taken into custody for the sake of the community and for his own sake.

In the same conversation, the agent told me that since there had been a connection made between David and Susie's disappearance, and David and the young woman who was murdered, they had gone back to the abandoned ranch where the young woman's remains had been found. "We took the place apart, hoping to find more clues," he explained. Everything they found had been sent to the Smithsonian Institute in Washington, D.C., to be examined by biologists and anthropologists. This agent-in-charge, who had become a dear friend, now had to inform me, with great sorrow, "This morning, Marietta, we received a report that in the last parcel sent there was a bone positively identified as being part of the backbone of a young female child."

This was the physical proof of what I had already come to know in my heart and mind. How desperately I had wanted to believe David when he said on the phone that Susie was still alive. Deep inside, I had clung stubbornly and stead-fastly to the hope that some wild and unpredictable twist of events would suddenly reveal Susie alive and well and return her to my arms. Now I had to accept the fact that her life in this world had ended months ago.

I knew how sick David was. I knew the horrible circumstances of the young woman's death. Furthermore, I'd had fifteen months of learning to live without Susie's presence in our lives. I'd finally learned to set the dinner table without a place for her. I'd learned not to watch for her when the school bus stopped on our street. I'd learned to count four heads, not five.

That night, sleep was impossible for my anguished soul. I didn't have a tear left to cry, and, by God's grace, I didn't have a drop of anger to vent. Too restless to stay in bed, I pulled myself to my feet, marveling that there was no blood on the floor! Surely a human heart could not withstand this kind of agony without breaking. My precious little girl was safe in the arms of her heavenly Father, but I would never again hold her in mine, not in this world. Someday, in eternity, we would be reunited, but for now her lovely little face was gone from my sight. I had known that this sacrifice might be asked of me, and I would not argue with God any more; but the cost in pain and grief seemed to be more than I could bear.

I was standing alone in my bedroom, my face buried in my hands, immersed in anguish, bereft of all capacity to cope or hope. When I finally lifted my head, my eyes fell upon a scriptural calendar hanging nearby. Groping for something on which to focus, and out of sheer habit, I searched out the accompanying verse for that particular day. It was Psalm 126:5: "Those who sow in tears shall reap with songs of joy." My mind grasped it like the lifeline it was, given to me by God. I knew that my Father understood to what depths the sword of sorrow had pierced my heart, yet I was being called, even now, to "sow" with Him. Those words were His promise to me that He would redeem this tragedy as I cooperated with Him in accomplishing the purposes for which it was allowed.

I knew that it was not God's will that any suffering should ever come to His little ones, but He had allowed this, as He had allowed His own Son's death, and I could trust that Susie was so precious in His sight that none of her suffering, or mine, would be for naught. Our Father could and would bring new life from it all. While Susie truly celebrated Life, He would enable me to "reap with songs of joy"!

14

Done—Yet Just Begun

The next morning, out in Montana, David was charged with the kidnap/murder of both Susie and the young woman and was incarcerated in the county jail. Although his arrest was without incident, he continued to insist he was innocent.

We were flooded with requests for interviews from television and press reporters, but we had to decline. I was a prime witness and had been cautioned not to discuss the case publicly. This was a difficult time for me to be quiet as a few reporters simply presumed vindictiveness on my part and reported so. I had to trust that God eventually would correct any wrong impressions.

The day after the arrest, the F.B.I. obtained search warrants for David's trailer and his other properties. Inside his home they found sheets with human bloodstains and other irrefutable evidence in his freezer.

At that time in the state of Montana the punishment for the crime of kidnap/murder was the death penalty. While it had not served as a deterrent for David, it was used now as a bargaining tool. David was confronted with the results of the search and was promised that if he made a full confession, he would not receive the death penalty, but would instead receive life imprisonment with a chance for psychiatric help. This had been my prayer for him, and because he could not deny the convicting evidence found in his home, David accepted the offer.

The Lost Child

With calm control, he now confessed to taking Susie's life, the life of the eighteen-year-old girl, and the lives of two young boys, in separate instances, a few years previously. One of these was the boy we had heard about when Susie was first taken—he had been stabbed to death in that same campground. David also revealed where Susie's skull was buried. The next morning, her few remains were recovered from the abandoned ranch.

A few hours after David had completed his confession, the officer bringing him his breakfast asked, "How's it going?" David replied, "Not so good!" Shortly thereafter, David committed suicide by hanging himself in his jail cell.

When the agent in charge of the case in Michigan called to notify us of David's death, all I could say was, "Oh, no! Oh, no! Oh, no!" over and over again. Only God knew what thoughts were in David's mind and heart in his last moments of life. All I could do was hope that in that last instant David received the ever-present mercy of the Lord and now lived with Him. I could only pray that for all eternity he was now healed and whole.

With David's death, the case was resolved. All the loose ends could be tied up. The reward fund set up in Michigan by Susie's godparents was dissolved; all the money was returned to the many generous people who had donated it. Money which had been sent anonymously and thus could not be returned, approximately $1,150, was sent in Susie's name to St. Jude's Children's Research Hospital in Memphis, Tennessee, a facility for children with potentially terminal diseases.

The reward fund which had been set up by a Montana newspaper was given to the Montana Department of Justice's Law Enforcement Academy in Bozeman, Montana, to help establish a library. We are most honored that this facility has been named the Susan Jaeger Memorial Library.

Because, in reality, Susie was already buried in Montana, it seemed incongruous to have a funeral in Michigan. So in October, 1974, sixteen months after she was taken from us, Bill and I quietly traveled back to Montana to finally lay Susie to rest. Our dear friend, the agent in charge of the investigation, had made all the arrangements for us, and everything was in readiness when we arrived.

Knowing that someday Susie would have a glorious new body was a consolation as Bill and I stood there alone in the funeral parlor in front of the tiny infant-sized coffin that contained the few earthly remains of our beloved youngest daughter. Nonetheless, I was grateful we'd decided to leave the other children home in Michigan, as this final reminder of the physical realities surrounding her death was, as I had feared, almost too much for us to bear.

Because the facts were so atrocious, in helping our children deal with Susie's death we had felt it necessary to direct their focus to the spiritual reality of her continuing, but new life in heaven. Most of them were simply too young yet to have to handle some of the explicit details of her fate. The day would come soon enough for them to know, although we were careful to answer all their questions and give them every opportunity to "talk it out" and cry out their pain in our arms. I continue to pray for God's healing in all their memories of this whole experience.

What do people do who do not have the promise of eternal life in Jesus? How do people cope with the brutal death of a beloved child if "that's all there is"? What do they hold onto if they won't believe in a loving Father who wants to, and is more than able to, compensate for any and all suffering in this world? I only know that as we drove to the cemetery, I needed all the hope and promises I could find! I was so grateful that Jesus had made them available to me, and I clung to them with all the faith I had.

At our request, the only ones present were the funeral

director and a priest, pastor of the F.B.I. agent in charge of the investigation. This man of God, who had graciously consented to serve us on this most sorrowful occasion, had himself endured great personal suffering and tragedy, his own family being massacred before his eyes in his native country by Communist soldiers after World War II. Standing closely between him and Bill as he led us in prayer over Susie's coffin, I drew strength and peace from this good and kind man.

Yet, there was still a part of me that wanted to run as far away as I could get—my grief was so great at the sight of that tiny box. At that moment I really could appreciate Mary, standing at the foot of the cross, unable to alleviate the suffering of her beloved child, able only to stand in faith and hope with Him. I understood that my call was much the same now, and if I could stand in faith with Jesus in the presence of Susie's suffering and death, resurrection would come here, too. I had to keep reminding myself that it had already come for Susie, and it would come someday for me.

Isaiah 40:11 says, "He tends his flock like a Shepherd: He gathers the lambs in his arms and carries them close to his heart; he gently leads those that have young." I was without my "young,"; my Susie, my lamb, was in His arms now; my Shepherd would not abandon me. He would lead me to new life, too. Knowing that helped me to surrender Susie for the last time. Montana's Indian-summer sun was warm upon us as we walked away from our daughter's grave.

The next day I visited David's mother. David had been a loving and respectful son; his initiative and industriousness had put him on the road to becoming a successful businessman, and his mother was proud of him. She told me that as a young teen-ager he had made a profession of faith in Christ as his Savior. That information helped to restore joy to my heart. I knew the Lord would somehow be faithful to that early commitment as David met Him in eternity. The outcome of his life had been a terrible shock to her, and she was desperately trying to understand and accept the reality of what had happened, as well as bear the suffering and problems it brought. Human nature being what it is, some people assumed an attitude of "guilty by association" toward David's family. Needless to say, it was an extremely difficult and painful time for all of them. I was apprehensive that my visit would upset his mother, but she welcomed me graciously and we shared a special time together.

After contacting the other victim's parents and sharing grief, comfort, and the promise of prayers, it was time to go home. Everything was finally done—I thought. But the Lord had just begun to work in me.

15

Of Lambs and New Life

Life became normal again. Bill and the children and I resumed our regular activities. But now that I didn't have to concentrate all my energies on the outcome of Susie's disappearance, I had time to ponder all that had happened.

First of all, I was not the same woman I had been sixteen months ago. The impenetrable darkness of that night Susie disappeared was a graphic illustration of where I was then spiritually—in the dark, groping to see and understand with the little light I had, frightened, in the presence of evil and experiencing a terrible separation. And that hour that I desperately waited for the sun to rise seemed to be a concentrated experience of the longing of the "God-shaped vacuum" in all of us. As I looked back now and remembered how I had begged God to send the sun so I could see, so I now understood how my whole being had needed the Son, "the light of men. The light [that] shines in the darkness" (John 1:4—5).

And just as the sun did rise and shed light over the campground, so "for you who revere my name, the sun of righteousness will rise with healing in its wings" (Mal. 2:2). Slowly, thoroughly, and surely Jesus had healed my grief-stricken heart and given me new life, strong and secure in Him.

I had struggled to understand those verses that say, "The angel of the Lord encamps around those who fear him, and he delivers them" (Ps. 34:7), and, "No harm will befall you, no disaster will come near your tent. For he will command his angels concerning you to guard you in all your ways" (Ps. 91:10–11). I had been taking those words of Scripture literally, and they had not been true for us. However, now I began to realize that in the sense that my heart, my spirit, (my "tent," where I really dwell), had been guarded and kept safe from destruction by the evil one, those words were most certainly true!

I could remember that night in Montana so long ago when I was filled with hate and a desire for revenge, yet was called to surrender all those ugly feelings to God. How I had resisted! Now how grateful I was that He'd been so persistent; now I enjoyed a peace and joy I never dreamed possible. Furthermore, I could now see that He had truly answered every petition I made that night: "Please enable me not only to forgive this man with my lips, but to love him with my heart . . . let me be involved with the resolution . . . and if something terrible has happened, help me to understand why."

Not only had I been enabled to forgive David with my lips in a personal encounter, not just to a voice on the phone, but I also had come to love David, to have compassion for him, to be concerned for him, to understand his pain and loneliness and sickness. On my own, the most I could rouse was the willingness to have those feelings, but God made them a reality in me by working a miracle in my heart.

Also, God had permitted me to be part of the resolution of Susie's disappearance. It was only because of the phone calls David made to me that his identity was positively determined and his arrest made possible. The investigative work of the F.B.I. and sheriff's department was absolutely essential and invaluable, but God had also ordained that I would be a major participant.

Finally, I recalled the last petition I made that night: "If You have allowed something terrible to happen to Susie, please help me to understand why." The answer to this prayer is still coming, in many and various ways. To me, the first obvious reason was that Susie was chosen by God and marked in the womb by her fingernails to be one of His special lambs, a sacrificial lamb to give her life so that other children could live.

David was very, very sick, and in his sickness would have continued to kill children. There was overwhelming evidence to this fact. He needed to be identified, and it was through the investigation of Susie's disappearance that this became possible. He had never called any other parent of those whose lives he'd taken. Even when he was suspected, he'd been able to pass the ordinary tests devised by man. David presented a threat of death to the children of that community. Susie's death was, in effect, a gift of life for them. Though Susie had to suffer grievously, now she was safe in the arms of her heavenly Father, living a glorious new life!

And through this measure of understanding, I began to understand how God was answering my plea to know more about Jesus. For Jesus was the perfect sacrificial Lamb of God, called from the womb, whose death was a gift of life for humanity. He, too, suffered grievously, but now He reigned in glory at the right hand of His Father.

I needed to see the parallel in the "benefit" of Susie's death to the community to understand what Jesus had done for me. I was still striving to remove the threat of evil and death by my own efforts "to be good," and failing miserably. What freedom it gave me to know that Jesus had already done it! Just as those children in Montana now could relax from their fears and enjoy the lives that lay before them; all that was needed from me was the willingness to give myself fully to all the possibilities of this new life in Jesus Christ.

Another parallel in Susie's story which taught me about Jesus concerned the ransom demanded for her return. You will recall that when we were so desperately seeking some way to raise the ransom money after David's first call, a man had come forth, a stranger to us but a friend of a friend who lived in neither Michigan nor Montana. Requesting that he remain anonymous to us, this man deposited fifty thousand dollars in a special bank account to be used as payment for Susie's ransom. He stipulated that if we were able to use it, we would *never* have to pay him back. *It was pure gift.* He would be grateful to know he'd been able to help save a child's life. All he asked of us was that we pray for him.

We could hardly believe it! Who, in this day and age of utilitarian values for life, would give fifty thousand dollars to absolute strangers with no desire to be repaid? Even as I write this years later, I continue to pray for this man in gratefulness for his incredible generosity in our time of utter need. May he always be blessed by the God whose generosity cannot be outdone! I hope by now he will know how much his selfless act helped me to really understand the ransom Jesus paid for all of us.

For truly, all of humanity was separated from the Father and totally incapable of bringing themselves back to Him. Then Jesus came along and freely gave Himself as ransom. In no way did any of us merit that; in no way can we pay it back. But merit and repayment are not required. All we need do is receive it with grateful hearts. It is *pure gift,* and it is always "on deposit," waiting to be used. "Yahweh Himself ransoms the souls of His servants, and those who take shelter in Him have nothing to pay" (Ps. 34:22 JB).

I know how we ached to be able to pay for Susie's safe return, and in that I know that I've been given a glimpse into the heart of God as He waits for each of us. How much more does He ache to bring His children home to the safety of His arms. So much so, that He allowed His own Son to die! When Susie's disappearance was resolved, it was a special consolation to us that other children would benefit from her death. However, had we known before we went to Montana that our little girl would have to sacrifice her life so that other children could live, we'd never have left Michigan! We didn't love the people of Montana that much! There's no way we'd have put Susie through that kind of ordeal or required that of ourselves. Yet that's how much God loves us. He knew what would happen to His Son whom He loved, and still He sent Him to earth to sacrifice His life so that we could have the eternal life He had created us to have.

We really undermine and underestimate the suffering of Jesus and *the cost to God* of allowing that suffering. It's as if there's a part of us that says that Jesus was God and therefore everything wasn't as bad as it looked. But Jesus was fully human. He had to walk in complete faith and a growing awareness of who He was, just as we do; He felt His sufferings at least as much as any other human being, and His Father did not intervene.

We are appalled to think of horrible crimes committed against innocent children such as Susie, but Jesus was utterly innocent, too. His holiness and goodness were ever unmatched; yet He was required to lay down His life and accept death as a common criminal to see that God's justice was done. I have said earlier in this book that God's idea of justice is not punishment but restoration. In Jesus, life as God originally intended it has been restored. "In faithfulness he will bring forth justice; he will not falter or be discouraged till he establishes justice on earth" (Isa. 42:3–4). But it came at a terrible price!

Because of His sinlessness and complete vulnerability we may never comprehend the enormity of Jesus' suffering, but suffer He did, in every possible way. All He had to hang onto, as He gave in to apparent defeat and failure and the darkness of death, was the promise of His Father's love—that the Father would not fail Him nor forsake Him. And, of course, the Father did not. But He allowed Jesus, His Son, to endure the seeming annihilation of His whole person so that *He could bring forth the First-born* of many sons and daughters. The torture of the Cross had to be endured, and God allowed His Son to do just that—the Son whom He dearly loved, the Son whom He cherished—so that we might see in Jesus how the Father loves, be reconciled with Him, and have true Life. That's how much God loves us.

As a parent whose daughter's suffering and death has been allowed, I cannot imagine loving anyone else enough to make that sacrifice for their benefit, but that's what our Father has done for us. I can only fall to my knees in the face of that inestimable gift.

How does one say "thank you" for a gift like that? There is something in me that always wants to repay gifts and favors. For a long time, I felt I had to do something for God. I kept searching out "good works" in which to serve Him and thereby pay back my debt. It took Him a while to break through my bullheaded determination to "do" and convince me that His first concern was just for me to "be," to live fully the life that had been made possible for me—life in the kingdom of God as a daughter of the King!

And His Spirit in us makes possible "kingdom living" in the *here and now* of this world. In His example and His words, Jesus gave us principles and attitudes by which we are to live and love. However, with our broken and weak human natures, we fail again and again. He who created us knew that we would, and that's why He sends His Spirit to live within us. He is too kind and merciful to give us commandments to follow and then leave us helpless to do so. But in the power of the Holy Spirit, the life of God in us, we can "be" all that God created us to be and, consequently, "do" all that He desires of us.

Through Susie's suffering, I really came to understand the difference between living "in the world" and living "in the Spirit." On my own, I would never have even desired to forgive David, let alone work toward it; but with the Spirit of God living within me, I was enabled not only to forgive David, but to come to love him. I was empowered by the Holy Spirit to love and forgive as I let Him be Lord in my heart.

The Holy Spirit is the person of the Trinity who brings order out of chaos. It is the Spirit who can re-create our hearts so that we grow daily in the image of our oldest brother, Jesus. It is the Spirit who empowers us to live as true sons and daughters of the King.

God's Holy Spirit has made the difference between life and death in my own spirit. I may still argue and resist and struggle and even fall—but the potential and power to be all that God calls me to be is there by the presence of the Holy Spirit living within.

16

The Parable of Susie

Being the youngest child, during her preschool years Susie was home alone with me while the others attended school; she spent many hours with me working in the kitchen, singing and laughing, reading stories, and having picnic lunches in the backyard. I loved being with her, and she loved being with me. She was a lively, bouncy, normal little girl.

However, during the last six months of her life, Susie became more concerned about what she could do for others—to a marked degree. Her behavior was obviously influenced by this uncommon attitude. She delighted in doing favors for all of us, in giving gifts, in making people "happy."

Once, shortly before we went to Montana, I had been working outside all day, digging and planting our garden, hoping to get it all done before we left. I was dirty and tired when I came in and plunked myself down in a chair, trying to get up enough energy to put a meal together for my family. Just then Susie walked in and asked if she could wash my feet. I was appalled that she wanted to do such a thing! Certainly I could step into the bathtub and wash all the garden grime off myself. There was no need for her to do it for me.

But she begged and begged, saying, "Just sit there and rest, mama, till I'm done. You'll feel lots better. . . . I finally relented, just to stop her fussing. So, laying a towel under my feet, she happily washed them in a pan of warm, soapy water. After drying them, she applied a soothing lotion and then sprinkled them with cologne. Her joy in being able to do this for me made it well worth the embarrassment I felt. And she was right—I did feel "lots better" and sufficiently rested to begin preparing dinner.

Now, that memory of Susie washing my feet has particular significance for me. But at the time, I appreciated it only as another of Susie's loving ways, of which she had many. And one day, after she was kidnapped and before the case was solved, I was inundated with the remembrance of all those loving ways. Everywhere I looked I saw her—her happy face at the kitchen table, sitting with Bill in the living room, rubbing her daddy's neck and shoulders in the car as he drove, skipping across the lawn, playing with her best friend across the street. No matter how I tried to distract myself, I could not shake loose the vivid memories of Susie. Oh, how I missed her! My loneliness was almost more than I could bear. Finally, too weary to resist any longer, I shut myself in my bedroom and just let the tears flow.

"Oh, Father," I prayed, "please forgive me; I'm not complaining. I'll wait as long as You need me to. But I love her so! Her presence in my life gave me such joy, and my arms ache just to hold her again. Even if someone else is being good to her, I know we belong together. Wherever she is, no one can love her like I do; no one knows what's best for her like I do; no one can care for her like her own mother."

As I struggled to communicate how I felt and thereby get my feelings in perspective and under control, suddenly I felt the presence of the Lord come near me. It seemed as if He was sitting at my side, comforting me. I sensed very clearly His utter sympathy, His total understanding of my loss. Then—the emphasis seemed to shift from my heartache to His, and I found myself caught up in an anguish that was more than I could bear: the anguish our Father feels because

His children have been taken from *His* arms. It was my own grief magnified over and over, and I was undone by the experience of it, especially as I realized I myself had been responsible for causing my Father to endure that pain again and again.

My first reaction was that I was unworthy to live; my mind immediately began to search for a way to take my own life. Just as swiftly, though, I realized that my suicide would make His anguish permanent. I recognized that the only way I could assuage His pain in any way would be to completely and unconditionally surrender my life to Him. More specifically, I wanted to offer myself as an instrument to help bring His other lost children back. Just as there were many people working to find Susie for us, I desired now to serve my Father in His effort to bring His children home. For I had experienced on a human level what our Father experiences to a degree our finite minds cannot comprehend. And if, through reading my story, you have been able to share my anguish, my grief, my loss, then you, too, have been given a glimpse into the heart of God as He grieves for His kidnapped children.

There are those who feel the idea of God grieving is an incongruity, even an impossibility—how can God, who has and is everything good, grieve? Yet, to love is to make oneself vulnerable to grief, and God has chosen to create and love us; surely He cannot rejoice when His children are suffering and dying, and that is our fate when we are separated from Him—who is the very source of life. As He loves His children, so does He long for their company. Only He knows how to care for them best. His children bring Him great joy, and He knows that they *need* to be with Him to live. If I grieved for my child taken from me, then He, the greatest Parent, who is the author of my mother's heart, surely grieves for His children.

The Lost Child

Thus, I offered and committed myself that day, knowing that the Lord Himself had placed that desire in my heart and was calling me, knowing He would lead and guide me in this work. After Susie's disappearance was solved and I began to share her story and mine with others, I realized that this was the medium which the Lord wanted me to use to reach His lost children. This book, then, has been written as part of my attempt to be faithful and obedient to His call as I understand it thus far.

And so I come to the primary reason I have chosen to share this entire experience with you. It is to this end, I believe, that God allowed Susie to be taken; it is the redemptive result of God working through evil. Throughout the Old Testament there are many references to God's tent, His dwelling-place among His people. In the beginning, this actually was a tent, constructed by Moses according to the Lord's instructions. Later it became a permanent structure, the temple built by Solomon. The tent-temple was where, in time and space, God dwelt with His people and where His people came together to meet and be with God and share in His life. In the New Testament, Jesus becomes God's dwelling-place among all people. John 1:14, translated literally says, "The Word became flesh and pitched His tent among us." Now Jesus sits at the right hand of the Father and we—the people of God, the Christian church—are called to be God's dwelling-place, God's tent, among all people.

Just as Susie was taken away from her father's tent, many of God's children have been taken away from His tent; and my grief and yours, as you have shared my experience, are the means our Father wants to use to help us know *how deeply He is grieving* for *His* kidnapped children and how He longs for their return. We need to realize that *many of us* are His kidnapped children. That may come as a surprise, because, like Susie, we think we are "safe in our Father's tent"—worshiping God, doing good works, giving money to the poor, taking care of our responsibilities, trying to live Christian lives. But somehow, the ways of the world have crept in, and we've been kidnapped by an unforgiving spirit. Someone has hurt us or a loved one, and because we've really suffered from that, we've not forgiven that person. So regardless of how good a life we live, how often we pray or go to church, how much we do for others, we are not in the safety of our Father's tent, we are *not* in a good relationship with God.

We pray, "Forgive us our trespasses (our sins) as we forgive those who trespass (sin) against us." In other words, we agree that our sins won't be forgiven unless we forgive those who sin against us. Jesus Himself said, "If you forgive men when they sin against you, your heavenly Father will also forgive you. But if you do not forgive men their sins, your Father will not forgive your sins" (Matt. 6:14–15).

If we are harboring an unforgiving spirit, no matter what the circumstances, we are not in our Father's tent—we are not in good relationship with Him. Our sin separates us from God. "Surely the arm of the Lord is not too short to save, nor his ear too dull to hear. But your iniquities have separated you from your God; your sins have hidden his face from you, so that he will not hear" (Isa. 59:1–2).

Vengeance, hatred, resentment, grudge-bearing, even deliberate indifference, are death-dealing spirits that will take our lives as surely as Susie's was taken from her. They *will* destroy us physically, mentally, emotionally, and spiritually. The world is full of people suffering debilitating, crippling, devastating diseases of mind and body, many of which stem from unforgiveness. More and more members of the healing professions are discovering the need to treat the whole person because attitudes and feelings buried deep within the inner self are often responsible for the problems and illnesses of the outer self. Unforgiveness takes an unbearably heavy toll and *ends in death, one way or the other.*

Yet often we don't even recognize the unforgiveness in ourselves because we've lived with it so long; and even if we do, we feel justified in it. We feel it is a righteous reaction because we or those we love have truly suffered, whether it be by an alcoholic parent, unfaithful spouse, incorrigible child, dishonest associate, corrupt government official, cruel neighbor, rebellious student, disloyal friend, wanton criminal—the list goes on as long as there are people. Conversely, it may also result from a minor situation, seemingly such an insignificant irritation or even necessary aggravation in our everyday lives that we fail to acknowledge the presence of unforgiveness in our hearts because of its constancy.

Certainly the attitudes of the world, the feelings of our flesh, and Satan's promptings support those kinds of reactions and would have us believe that forgiveness is foolish, cowardly, unreasonable, unjust, outrageous, unnecessary, irresponsible, and/or impossible because it is contrary to our human nature.

But God wants us to live, and so He calls us to forgive, again and again if we must, so that He can forgive us again and again if He must, absolutely and unconditionally as He does. He calls us to die to ourselves, to take up our cross daily, and by that He means to be willing to give up all those attitudes that are contrary to His and to be willing to let His Spirit give us His life, His heart, His mind. The prophet Micah says, "Who is a God like you. Who pardons sin and forgives the transgression. . . . You do not stay angry forever but delight to show mercy" (Mic. 7:18). That is what we are called to as Christians.

Certainly there is a price to pay. It cost Jesus His life. It is important that we are fully aware of the cost of our forgiveness. Satan will work overtime reminding us, attempting to undermine or deter our efforts and intentions, but it will serve God's purpose anyway. We will be better able to carry out the forgiveness to which we are called if we understand exactly what is being required in each of our own circumstances. We *can* trust that God will be our *justice*, our *defense*, our *recompense*. *He is more than capable, and He is always faithful*.

As long as we remain with our Father, we are asked to work in the "family business"; we are called to follow our oldest brother, Jesus, in the ministry of reconciliation. God is the Lord of history, and there is no one in any of our lives whom He has not allowed to be there. He wants us to remove any obstacle in our relationships with others so that His love can flow through us to them.

Jesus told His disciples: "I tell you the truth, whatever you bind on earth will be bound in heaven, whatever you loose on earth will be considered loosed in heaven" (Matt. 18:18). That applies to us also; we, too, are His disciples. As we are willing to love and forgive others as needed, God's love can reach them and accomplish in their hearts what needs to be done, in His way and in His time, because we have not bound them up, as well as ourselves, by our unforgiveness. As we work with Jesus to restore unity and wholeness on the earth, we ourselves become healed and healthy, holy and whole.

But even holy and whole persons with the best of intentions can offend one another. We all come from different temperaments, backgrounds, cultures. We respond to life in different ways, often hurting another despite our desire to do good. Even without malice, our words and actions can alienate and cause dissension and division. But the Spirit of God seeks to bring unity and peace, to make us one in Jesus, one body, one family of God. *Forgiveness is the key to this unity and peace—as it is practiced daily in the lives of Christians living in the power of God's Spirit.*

I know it is not easy. In fact, it is very difficult. The price I had to pay, the anguish I had to bear, at times seemed intolerable, interminable, and devastating. But forgiveness *is* possible.

At one point before the resolution of Susie's disappearance, shortly before the first anniversary call, you will recall I mentioned having a most horrible nightmare. In this terrifying dream I was an observer, unable to intrude, intervene, speak, or stop the dream; it was as if a horror movie was being shown to me by force.

I saw Susie being pulled out of the tent, strangled to the point of unconsciousness, and carried away by a man and put onto the seat of a truck. I saw her waking up; her throat hurt; she was disoriented, then frightened as she realized she was with a strange man in a strange vehicle. I saw her taken into a building, saw her terror mounting as she was undressed. I never saw the face of the person with her, but I saw what he did to her. I watched as Susie became hysterical and uncontrollable, screaming for us. Then I watched her face—her precious, beautiful, little face—become ugly and contorted as she was strangled to death in his frustration. Afterward, I saw her body decapitated and dismembered, the parts disposed of in various ways. Finally, I was allowed to waken, to be set free from this unbearable nightmare.

I sat up in bed, shaking and filled with revulsion at the horror I'd just witnessed, utterly undone by my inability to reach Susie, to help her, to save her. "Oh, Lord," I prayed, "thank You that this is only a dream. I know nothing like this would happen in real life. I know You would not allow such a terrible thing as this to happen to my little girl. I could never live with a reality like this. I could never forgive a reality like this. Thank You that this is only a dream."

But when David made his confession, I discovered that this, indeed, was the reality I had to live with and forgive. I know now that I did not have a dream, but a vision sent by God to insure my complete awareness of Susie's suffering. As horrible as it was, I needed to know all that happened. Now there's no one who can come to me and say, "Marietta, if you *really* knew what Susie had to endure, you wouldn't be able to forgive." I *know* what Susie had to endure, and now I can truly speak with authority as I proclaim that, with the Spirit of God living within us, *any* kind of forgiveness is possible.

I ask your forgiveness if I have offended or upset you with my description of this vision, but you need to know that reality when you hear me declare that I grieved as much when David died as I grieved for my Susie. You need to know the scope of healing and strength and mercy that God can work in the hearts of His children as they try to love and forgive as He calls them to. You need to know how He longs to work those kinds of miracles in your own hearts. You need to know that as He did this for me in the most horrible of circumstances, He *will* do it for you in *your* circumstances.

And we all need to recognize the graphic illustration symbolically represented in Susie's suffering and death: unforgiveness binds us, cuts off the breath we need to live, which is God's life within us, and violates, devastates, kills, and destroys our bodies, our whole beings. We *must* come back to the safety of our Father's tent!

Don't be concerned about how you would feel if your own child were kidnapped. It's been my experience that Satan will often try to sabotage the Holy Spirit's conviction in our heart by sidetracking us with those kinds of thoughts, and they are pointless. It is not at all likely you will ever have to deal with such a situation. All you need to be concerned about are the areas *in your own life* where you have been kidnapped by an unforgiving spirit, by an instance that hap-

119

pened long ago or even today, by something that happened once or something that happens regularly.

Ask the Lord to show you where that area is; it's His heart's desire to bring you back. After all, He allowed His Son to suffer and die so that you might know and receive His life and His love. Don't allow that precious "ransom" to be wasted. Pray for the grace to make a decision to forgive; make it an act of will—and it will come. Follow through on that decision with actions that declare your forgiveness; begin to pray for the person regularly. Don't worry about wrong or negative feelings; they will help you to better understand what is going on in your heart if you acknowledge and work through them *with* the Lord. As you give way to the Spirit of God within you, the right feelings will happen, in His way and in His time.

Our Father wants to bring all His children home. Jesus has "paid the ransom" with His life, that inestimable gift, and sends the Holy Spirit to empower us, to live deeply within us so that we can be a merciful, generous, and peaceful people, so that we can forgive with His forgiveness and love with His love. As we forgive, we are forgiven, our sin no longer separates us from God, and we are brought back to the safety of His tent, the body of Christ in this world. We are reconciled with our Father. Then we are truly able to enjoy God's fullest blessing, protection, guidance, and providence as we live out the good lives He desires for us—lives of hope, direction, fulfillment, and joy.

There's a passage in the Book of Isaiah which says, "Joy and gladness shall be found in her, thanksgiving and the sound of a song" (51:3 NAB). I love those wonderful words because that's the kind of life the Lord has given to me in exchange for my willingness to forgive David!

I won't tell you that I never miss Susie or never feel any more anguish because of her suffering. Just as Jesus still bore the scars of His wounds after he rose from the dead, so I still bear mine. So will you. But every time we meet Jesus at the cross, every time we have to crucify our wrong feelings and desires, *we will experience resurrection with Him*—a new life, rich and full beyond our wildest dreams, to be lived *in the here and now of this world* as we practice forgiveness. Our Father wants *all* His children to have lives filled with joy and gladness, thanksgiving and the sound of song!

Then finally, one by one, He will bring us home to Himself for all eternity, where we will be the people

who have come out of the great tribulation; they have washed their robes and made them white in the blood of the Lamb. Therefore, they are before the throne of God and serve him day and night in his temple; and he who sits on the throne will spread his tent over them. Never again will they hunger; never again will they thirst. The sun will not beat upon them, nor any scorching heat. For the Lamb at the center of the throne will be their shepherd; he will lead them to springs of living water. And God will wipe away every tear from their eyes (Rev. 7:14—17).

And the ransomed of the Lord will return. They will enter Zion with singing; everlasting joy will crown their heads. Gladness and joy will overtake them, and sorrow and sighing will flee away (Isa. 35:10).

Other Pickering Paperbacks

JONI

You will never forget . . . JONI

The unforgettable story of a young woman's struggle against quadriplegia and depression.

At the age of 17 Joni Eareckson was the victim of a diving accident that left her totally paralysed from the shoulders down. In seconds her entire life was changed from a state of vigorous activity and independence to an existence of total helplessness and dependence.

Each step of Joni's struggles to accept and adjust to her handicap and her bitter, desperate search for the meaning of life is revealed for the first time in this unforgettable autobiography.

The suffering she endured had its effect in every area of her life—it was not easy for Joni to overcome her bitterness, confusion, violent questionings and tears, and learn to trust a loving God who had allowed this to happen.

Today, still able to move only her neck and head, Joni Eareckson has developed into a skilful artist, using her mouth to guide her pen.

"Losing her anger at God made the difference between suicide at 17 and a life of strong purpose. The very irony of Joni Eareckson's story suggests the existence of a Someone designing destinies."

MARY DANIELS *Chicago Tribune*

ISBN 0 7208 0412 4

JONI—A STEP FURTHER

In July 1967, when she was 17, Joni Eareckson dived into Chesapeake Bay and broke her neck: since then she has been a quadriplegic, confined to life in a wheelchair. In her first book *Joni*, she told the story of her accident and her subsequent struggle to accept her handicap.

As a result of that first book, Joni received thousands of letters from readers who identified with her bouts of depression, despair, and loneliness—letters from hurting people all over the world. Out of this came a sense of responsibility to respond to others and, thus, this book.

"Today as I look back, I am convinced that the whole ordeal of my paralysis was inspired by God's love. I wasn't the brunt of some cruel divine joke. God had reasons behind my suffering, and learning some of them has made all the difference in the world."

ISBN 0 7208 0432 9

SPIRITUAL DEPRESSION

Are you *happy* in your Christian life?
Do you experience the freedom, power and joy which God promises His people?

If not, you may well be suffering from the common complaint of "spiritual depression".

In this book, which has brought encouragement to thousands of Christians, pastor and doctor Martyn Lloyd-Jones diagnoses the causes of spiritual depression and prescribes the practical cure. He shows how those who are discouraged or depressed can learn to cope with themselves, conquer their problem, and be renewed and restored to spiritual health and strength.

Pickering Paperbacks ISBN 0 7208 0205 9

SELECTED TO LIVE

Johanna-Ruth Dobschiner tells of a Jewish childhood ravaged by the Nazis, and of her own shocked witness to the total destruction of her family—even as she miraculously escaped the same fate. Barely a teenager, she was already an adept fugitive, one step ahead of her Nazi pursuers as she went underground, moving from one sympathetic Dutch family to another until the end of the war. Here is the story of a girl who was picked out from thousands of condemned people and selected to live. After reading this book, you too will realise that *YOU* are SELECTED TO LIVE.

Johanna-Ruth Dobschiner now fulfils the role of housewife in a Glasgow suburb. It was also in this city that she trained as a nurse in the Victoria Infirmary where she gained her RGN. As wife and mother of twin daughters, plus the larger family of all those whose lives touch hers, she counts it a privilege to live and serve.

ISBN 0 7208 0212 1